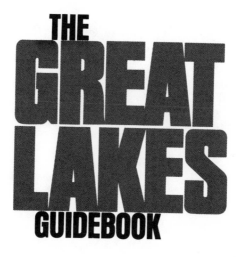

THE
GREAT
LAKES
GUIDEBOOK

George Cantor

THE GREAT LAKES GUIDEBOOK

Lake Superior and Western Lake Michigan

Ann Arbor   The University of Michigan Press

In Canada: John Wiley & Sons Canada, Limited

Library of Congress Cataloging in Publication Data

Cantor, George, 1941–   (Revised)
    The Great Lakes guidebook.

    Includes bibliographies and indexes.
    CONTENTS: [1] Lakes Ontario and Erie.—[2] Lake
Huron and eastern Lake Michigan.—[3] Lake Superior
and western Lake Michigan.
    1. Great Lakes region—Description and travel—Guide-
books. I. Title.
F551.C34 1978   917.7'0433   77–13606
ISBN 0–472–19650–2 (v. 1)

Contents

Maps

Introduction

The trip began on a chilly May morning in Port Stanley, Ontario—I was huddled inside my raincoat and doing my best to explore this old resort town on Lake Erie. It ended nearly two and a half years later on a biting cold September morning on a sightseeing boat in the Soo Canal. By now accustomed to the vagaries of Great Lakes weather and always prepared for the worst, I was again huddled inside my raincoat and saw what I could from the lounge; my wife remained smugly on deck wrapped in a warm red parka.

The Great Lakes trip had not been continuous. There were long breaks at home during which I sat absorbed over some arcane volume salvaged from local libraries that would give up a bit more information about these huge bodies of water. I had lived my entire life within an hour's drive of parts of their shorelines; not until these travels began, though, did I realize how little I knew about them.

At first the idea of writing a series of guidebooks to the Lakes seemed like a piece of cake. As a reporter and editor I had traveled extensively, including a dozen or so trips to Europe. During a previous incarnation as a baseball writer, I had been a frequent visitor to outposts like Cleveland, Chicago, and Milwaukee. I was a native of Detroit and had vacationed throughout Michigan. Within me was a vast repository of stored knowledge which simply had to be transferred to the printed page to make a book. So I thought.

As initial plans for the books progressed, though, I became frighteningly aware that I really knew next to nothing about this area. Cities I had driven through dozens of times were now like Arabian seaports—mysterious and unfathomable. I had no idea how they were born, developed, and assumed their present shape over the passage of years. A few facts dimly recalled from past history courses were all I had to go on. Obviously, this was going to be more than that piece of cake I had bargained for—more like a twelve-course banquet.

But as I researched and traveled along every mile of shore that a road can reach, I began to realize what a history this region has. As a child I had visited the ruins of Fort Malden in Amherstburg, Ontario—only one hour from Detroit—but I never understood, not really, the role these silent stones once played in a vicious and ludicrous war that had brought death and occupation to my own hometown. I had been raised on Western movies and was especially partial to those in which Indians and pioneers collided in gory combat, but I had never heard of the bloody drama that was played out near Lake Huron, at Ste. Marie-among-the-Hurons. The entire Huron nation and their Jesuit companions were eradicated there by the Iroquois, who were fighting a desperate war to keep the French from their lands. I had faintly heard of the Michigan Copper Country, in my native state but 500 long miles from home. What I hadn't known was that these Lake Superior lands were the scene of a mining rush bigger than the stampede to California for gold, and that they contained ghost towns as haunting as any in the country.

In essence, I had always felt vaguely that history was something that happened someplace else—at Plymouth Rock or Gettysburg, at New Orleans or the Little Big Horn, at Bunker Hill or Virginia City—but not in the Midwest, around the Great Lakes, so close to home. And this was understandable. Although Great Lakes history is a rich dramatic source, relatively few enduring works of fiction have been drawn from it. *The Song of Hiawatha* comes to mind, a little of James Fenimore Cooper, some of the Chicago writers, a few chronicles of Ontario pioneer life.

Just as important, the chief elements of popular culture—movies and television—have passed it by. Aside from the "Rainbow Country" series of the Canadian Broadcasting Company, not much has been done with the Lakes. This also is understandable. Lakes Indians were generally not horsemen, so there was no possibility of a wide-screen cavalry charge. The War of 1812, the main conflict that centered on the Lakes, was an important part of Canadian history but more of an embarrassment to the United States. So it, too, has been ignored. Although the histories of great cities like Chicago, Detroit, Toronto, Milwaukee, and Cleveland make absorbing reading, they do lack a certain glamour. There are a few movies about the Chicago fire, and the Lakes area serves as incidental background for a television series or two, but that's about it.

In the happy phrase of the entertainment industry, the inhabitants of this part of the country are the "flyover people." They are simply what is down there as one jets from New York to Los Angeles and back—not terribly bright (or else they'd be living in New York or Los Angeles), or terribly interesting, or terribly attractive. The entire Midwest can be written off as cornfields, factories, and rubes who think "Charlie's Angels" is the hottest thing since peanut butter. The Great Lakes, moreover, as everyone knows, are polluted sinkholes where no fish can survive and boats corrode upon contact. Better, by far, to depict once more the hills of golden California or the sidewalks of New York.

Thus, although this is primarily a guidebook, I also hope it can help bring alive some small part of the often ignored yet incredibly colorful history of the Lakes—either to those who live near them or to those who are making their first visit.

Each of the five Great Lakes has its own personality, a set of characteristics that are apparent to those who sail their waters or who spend any length of time on their shores.

Lake Superior is the largest body of fresh water on the globe. It covers an area larger than the state of Maine, a total of 31,800 square miles. Its scenery matches its size. Superior is rimmed by hills and rugged bluffs, the most spectacular landscapes on the Lakes and some of the grandest in the hemisphere. It is the *Gitche Gumee* of the Chippewa, the "laughing big sea water" of Longfellow's *Hiawatha*. But to the French it was *supérieur*. The bustling harbors at its western end—Duluth-Superior and Thunder Bay—send the freighters away full of grain and ore, making the lake a vital segment in the economy of two nations. These ports, however, are the only cities of any size on Superior's shores. Its largest island is Isle Royale, a United States national park and wilderness preserve. Other major geographic features are the Apostle Islands, Wisconsin, now a national lakeshore; the Pictured Rocks, also a national lakeshore, in Michigan; and the long, hooked arm of the ruggedly beautiful Keweenaw Peninsula of Michigan. The lake empties into the St. Marys River at the twin cities of Sault Ste. Marie. The Soo Locks there carry twice the traffic of the Panama Canal.

STATISTICS OF THE GREAT LAKES

Lakes	Length mi. km.	Breadth mi. km.	Size sq. mi. km.^{2}	Greatest Depth ft. m.	Largest Cities
Superior	350	160	31,800	1,333	Thunder Bay, Ontario
	560	*256*	*82,362*	*406*	Duluth, Minnesota
					Superior, Wisconsin
Huron	206	183	23,010	750	Sarnia, Ontario
	330	*293*	*59,595*	*229*	Port Huron, Michigan
					Bay City, Michigan
Michigan	307	118	22,400	923	Chicago, Illinois
	491	*189*	*58,016*	*281*	Milwaukee, Wisconsin
					Gary, Indiana
Erie	241	57	9,910	210	Cleveland, Ohio
	386	*91*	*25,667*	*64*	Buffalo, New York
					Toledo, Ohio
Ontario	193	53	7,550	802	Toronto, Ontario
	309	*85*	*19,555*	*244*	Hamilton, Ontario
					Rochester, New York

Lake Huron comes next, the lake first seen by Europeans but the one that has remained least developed. Samuel de Champlain reached its shores in 1615. He had worked his way from Montreal along the Ottawa River, overland to Lake Nipissing and then along the French River to its outlet at the lake. He took this rather circuitous route west because the hostile Iroquois controlled the southern approaches. The existence of Lakes Erie and Ontario was then only a vague rumor. Even with this head start, Huron has remained far from the most heavily traveled roads. The site at which Champlain first saw the lake remains inaccessible by automobile. Lake Huron's largest city, Sarnia, Ontario, has a population of about 60,000. The only other significant pocket of industry is concentrated on Saginaw Bay, which contributes whatever pollution the lake suffers. It is the second largest of the Lakes and the most irregularly shaped. Its massive eastern arm, Georgian Bay, is cut off from the rest of the lake by Manitoulin Island, the largest island on the Lakes. Other islands shield the North Channel. There are two units of Georgian Bay Islands National Park in Canada, one near Midland and the other at the tip of the slender Bruce Peninsula, near Tobermory. Mackinac Island, one of the stateliest resorts in the States, guards the western approach to Lake Huron at the Straits of Mackinac.

Lake Michigan is separated from Lake Huron only by a narrow strait. The two lakes lie at the same distance above sea level and are virtual twins in size. But Michigan is a lake with a split personality. At its southern end, unlike Huron, it supports one of the most intensive concentrations of industrial wealth and population in the world. Chicago, the pivotal metropolis of the Lakes, occupies its southwestern corner. The band of development continues eastward around the Calumet district of Indiana and northward to Milwaukee, another booming port and industrial center. But where the suburbs of the Wisconsin city end, the North begins, and Lake Michigan becomes a resort-studded jewel. Its waves lap at some of the richest vacation property in the Midwest. Green Bay, on the Wisconsin shore, has the Door Peninsula, and on the east the two Traverse Bays, Grand and Little, are lined with showplaces. Nearby is the Sleeping Bear Dunes National Lakeshore. Michigan is the only Great Lake entirely within the boundaries of the United States, but its largest island, Beaver, once was ruled by a king—albeit a self-proclaimed monarch.

The accumulated flows of Lakes Michigan and Huron empty into the St. Clair River at the cities of Sarnia and Port Huron. At the far end they flow into Lake St. Clair, a sort of Great Lake, junior grade. At 460 square miles it is somewhat bigger than a pond but not in the same league as its enormous neighbors. Its Canadian shoreline is mostly undeveloped; Walpole Island is occupied by an Indian reservation. Detroit's suburbs sprawl along its southwestern end. At Belle Isle it meets the Detroit

River, busiest inland waterway in the world and scene of industrialization beyond compare.

Lake Erie is the shallowest, busiest, oldest, and dirtiest of the Lakes. Sailors distrust it. The lake is shaped like a saucer, and when storms come out of the west it can be a treacherous body of water. One of these gales can cause a thirteen-foot difference in water level at opposite ends of the lake and raise waves of frightening size. With an average depth of just fifty-eight feet, Erie is also especially susceptible to industrial pollution. It has suffered more severely from pollution than any other lake; its southern shoreline is covered with major ports, from Toledo to Buffalo, and industrial discharges from Detroit alone almost succeeded in killing it. The lake is improving but is by no stretch of the imagination clean. Still, it supports major resort areas around Ohio's Sandusky Bay and the Presque Isle Peninsula of Pennsylvania. In contrast to the American shore, the Canadian side of Erie is almost empty, with only small resorts and fishing towns breaking the long stretches of solitude. Point Pelee and Long Point, both major wildlife sanctuaries and bird refuges, are the main landmarks. Pelee Island, largest in the lake, belongs to Canada and is primarily agricultural.

Erie empties into the churning Niagara River, which thunders over its escarpment a few miles on to form one of the world's great natural wonders. Just beyond Niagara Falls, the river passes through a tumultuous gorge before peacefully emerging into the last of the Lakes.

Lake Ontario is the least Great Lake, covering only 7,550 square miles, which is still a larger area than the state of New Jersey. But it is second deepest, with an average sounding of 283 feet. Its depth results in a strong moderating influence over the adjacent countryside's climate, and one of the great fruit belts of North America is situated around its littoral. The western end of the lake is Ontario's most densely populated region. Toronto, second largest city in the country, and Hamilton, one of Canada's greatest manufacturing centers, present a solid belt of intensive development. On the American side, however, Rochester is the only city of significant size. The shoreline is quite regular, with only the mass of Quinte's Isle breaking into the lake from the north. There are no islands of any size in Lake Ontario, aside from the farthest eastern corner. There Wolfe and Amherst, Ontario, guard the entrance to the St. Lawrence River at Kingston, eastern limit to the Lakes.

From Duluth, Minnesota, to Kingston, Ontario, it is a journey of 1,160 miles through the world's largest freshwater system, the largest inland water transportation network—the superlatives go on and on. You might consider this: the Great Lakes system contains sixty-seven trillion gallons of water, and much of it is even drinkable.

In terms of geological time, the Great Lakes are rank upstarts. They began taking shape about 18,000 years ago, the end product of North America's final age of glacial activity. It was called the Wisconsin Age, because the ice reached to what is now the southern limits of that state. As the glaciers started their long retreat, ancient stream valleys were uncovered and slowly began filling with meltwater and rain. Lakes formed in the area of Chicago and the Maumee Valley, both bodies of water draining into the Mississippi River. As the ice moved farther north the patterns changed. The lakes twisted into new shapes and sent their waters over newly formed drainage routes. Lake Erie and the southern portion of Lake Michigan had reached an approximation of their present forms about 10,000 years ago. Lake Ontario was shaped about 7,000 years ago. The Upper Lakes assumed their present outline a mere 3,000 years ago.

We have said previously that Champlain was the first European to see the Lakes, but that may not be strictly true. A shadowy figure named Étienne Brulé, sent out by Champlain to scout the area, may actually have reached the Lakes as early as 1612. It is hard to say. Brulé left no records. He was illiterate and was the first of the voyageurs to adapt successfully to the ways of the Indians. Eventually he was killed by them in the wilderness, after ranging from Lake Ontario to Isle Royale. He is, however, given credit for being the first European to see Lake Superior.

Twenty years after Champlain's expedition, Jean Nicolet explored Lake Michigan, reaching the site of Green Bay, Wisconsin. By 1631, two Jesuit priests, Fathers Jogues and Rambault, had established missions there and on Lake Superior, at Ashland,

Wisconsin, and the Soo. Not until 1669 was the last of the Lakes discovered. Louis Joliet and Robert LaSalle entered Lake Erie a few days apart that summer from opposite directions. In another four years, Joliet and Father Marquette would discover the route from the Lakes to the Mississippi River, and Fort Frontenac would be established as a permanent settlement at the mouth of the St. Lawrence River.

Finally, in 1679, LaSalle embarked on the crowning epic of Great Lakes discovery. Aboard his ship, the *Griffon*, he sailed across Erie, up the Detroit River and around Huron into Michigan, finally disembarking at Green Bay. The voyage opened up the southern route to the Upper Lakes and clarified the geographic relationship between the two segments. LaSalle went on to trace the Mississippi River to the Gulf of Mexico. The *Griffon* was sent home to Lake Erie, and on the way back it vanished. Several museums around the Lakes display bits and pieces of what is thought to be the wreckage of the ship. But that is only guesswork. No one knows what happened to the ship or exactly where it went down. On that mysterious note the great discoveries on the Lakes ended and the age of settlement began.

It took the War of 1812 to establish the boundary between the United States and Canada in the Great Lakes area. In 1817 the border was settled by the Rush-Bagot Agreement, and it has not been changed since.

Crossing this frontier is usually an uncomplicated, rapid procedure. No documents are required for citizens of either country, but it is advisable to carry some proof of citizenship, such as a copy of a birth certificate or voter registration card. Naturalized citizens should carry their certificates of naturalization and aliens must have their registration cards.

Motorists should have proof of car ownership and insurance coverage with them. Most personal items may be taken across the border without trouble, but rifles and expensive camera equipment should be registered at the border. No handguns are permitted in Canada.

Dogs may cross the border if their owners present a certificate that the animal has been vaccinated against rabies in the last year. A description of the animal must accompany the certificate. Cats may cross freely.

For complete customs information, the traveler should request information, in advance, from the Customs Office in either Washington, D.C., or Ottawa, Ontario.

All of which brings us to this book.

It has been my experience as a travel editor that travel books fall roughly into two major categories. There are the personalized books of essays and observations, which may be great fun to read but not much help when it comes right down to planning a trip. Then there are the nuts-and-bolts sorts of listings, which have all the facts and figures but are about as readable as the Yellow Pages.

I have tried to stake out a middle ground. It is my hope that the essays in this book are written in a manner that will entertain. But I also intend this book to be used as a planner and an on-the-road reference guide.

It is a selective guidebook. I have made no attempt to catalog every sight and attraction on the shoreline of the Great Lakes. I did endeavor, though, to list the best and most significant. They are the places that reflect the long and colorful history of the area, with appeal that is unique to the Lakes.

At the beginning of each chapter there is an introductory essay about the particular area being explored. It will examine some of the features that influenced the area's historical development and the special qualities that can be found there.

Offered next are three attractions that I have selected as being the best in the area. If you are traveling through, these are the things you should make a special effort to see. Some of them are among the best-known sights on the continent; others are rarely publicized outside their immediate locale. But they are all top-notch attractions. These three sights are discussed in depth, and several are accompanied by useful maps.

After that follows a section we have called "Other Things to See." They are listed in about the order in which you would encounter them if you were to drive across the area. A few of these sights are marked with boldface numbers. This indicates that while they do not quite rank with the "Top Three" in the area, they are nonetheless unusually worthwhile and significant attractions. The others on the list can be seen during a stay of a few days in the area or may appeal to special interests. Some area maps in this section have accompanying maps showing greater detail of the major cities in the area not otherwise visible in the overall map.

Then, frequently, a section called "Side Trips," suggesting interesting things to see within a fifty-mile drive of the lakeshore, is presented. Finally, there is a list of major state and provincial parks in the area, especially those with lakefront recreational facilities. If overnight camping is permitted, the number of tent sites is given.

That, in brief, is our book.

Read it and enjoy it. Most of all, use it.

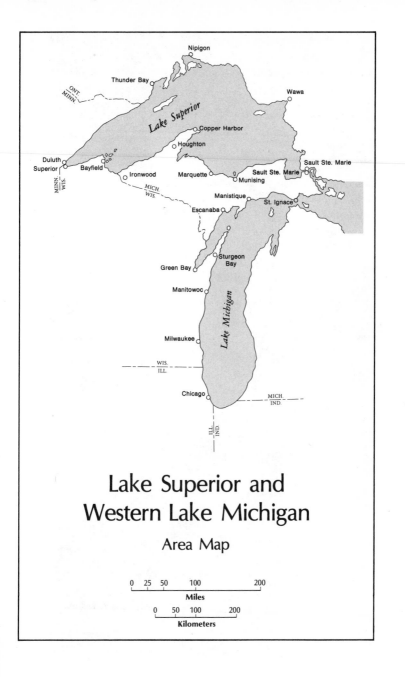

Nipigon

Thunder Bay

ONT.
MINN.

Wawa

Lake Superior

Copper Harbor

Houghton

Duluth
Superior

Bayfield

Ironwood

Marquette

Sault Ste. Marie

Sault Ste. Marie

MINN.
WIS.

Munising

MICH.
WIS.

Manistique

Escanaba

St. Ignace

Green Bay

Sturgeon
Bay

Manitowoc

Lake Michigan

Milwaukee

WIS.
ILL.

Chicago

MICH.
IND.

ILL.
IND.

Lake Superior and
Western Lake Michigan

Area Map

```
0   25  50      100              200
|___|___|_____|_____|
           Miles

    0    50  100     200
    |_____|___|_____|
         Kilometers
```

The Soo Locks, connecting Lake Superior with Lake Huron, carry twice the traffic of the Panama Canal. *Courtesy Travel Bureau, Michigan Department of Commerce.*

1

The Soo

The whole thing was beyond the understanding of Henry Clay. For what seemed like the hundredth time, the Congress of the United States was being asked in 1852 to approve an appropriations bill for a ship canal to be built at Sault Ste. Marie, Michigan. For thirteen years the state of Michigan had been trying to persuade Washington to assist in the construction of this canal. And the great statesman from Kentucky, a spokesman for the West during his entire public career, could not see the reason for it to save his soul. Clay rose during the debate on the project to protest. "It is a work beyond the remotest settlement of the United States," he said, "if not the moon."

But within a decade, the canal beyond the moon was to become the fulcrum of the country's industrial system, the stimulus to a rate of growth that would turn an agricultural nation into a world power. Iron and copper already had been discovered in northern Michigan; even richer lodes soon would be found in Minnesota. The ore would be funneled to the factories and markets of the East and Midwest through the Soo. In a few more years, grain from the great wheat fields of the Northwest would join the flow through these locks. In 1855, the year the

13

canal opened, 193 ships made the passage. In fifteen years that number had increased ten times, and by 1895 traffic was ten times again as great. By the 1970s, more than 100 million tons of cargo went through the Soo Locks annually, making them the busiest in the world by far.

Sault Ste. Marie already was an old city when the locks opened. The place was known to the French as early as 1641, and there are those who think the shadowy adventurer Étienne Brulé had visited a good twenty years before that. It dates its formal beginnings, though, from 1668, when Fr. Jacques Marquette founded a mission there, making it the oldest continuously inhabited settlement on the Great Lakes. *Sault* is the French word for rapids. The city grew around the nineteen-foot drop of the St. Marys River, the strait that connects Lake Superior and the lower Great Lakes. It was a natural spot for settlement. All goods passing through had to be unloaded and portaged around the falls. To the explorers it was a focal point of the Great Lakes. France chose the Soo in 1671 as the site for the ceremonies by which it took formal possession of the western lakes, a solemn event that astonished a few dozen Indian witnesses and made New France feel that the proper protocol had been observed.

The fur traders followed their customary policy of discouraging extensive settlement, but in 1750 a nobleman, the Sieur de Repentigny, was granted 214,000 acres in the vicinity by Louis XIV. To solidify his claim he fortified the Soo, but his bastion was captured twelve years later by the British. Repentigny refused to accept the result of the French and Indian War and fought for the colonials during the American Revolution rather than swear allegiance to Britain. The Americans didn't occupy the Soo, however, until 1820, and Repentigny's claims were never recovered. His descendants took their case all the way to the United States Supreme Court before being turned down finally in 1867.

Under British rule the Soo became a small fur trading outpost of the Montreal-based Northwest Company. Their representative, John Johnston, settled in with his bride, the daughter of an Ojibwa chief, and he is regarded as the first English-speaking resident. But when Johnston arrived in 1793, British days were already numbered. The Treaty of Paris had fixed the international boundary at the St. Marys River, and the south side was to pass under American control. Johnston had observed the inefficiency of the portage system around the falls and decided that a small canoe canal was needed. He also felt it would be best to build it on the northern side of the river, outside of the forthcoming American control. The canal opened in 1798 and was the first at the Soo, but it lasted only sixteen years. American raiders destroyed it during the War of 1812. They also burned down the home of Johnston, who remained a loyal British subject even though living in what was nominally American territory. Johnston, probably the wealthiest man in the North before the war, tried for years to collect reimbursement, first from the British and later from the American government, for the loss of his property. He was unsuccessful. His wife, though, remained firmly on the American side. She assisted Lewis Cass when he arrived in 1820 to raise the United States flag over the Soo and eventually married her daughter to Indian agent Henry Schoolcraft.

Three years after Cass's arrival, the military established Fort Brady at the Soo. The riverfront fort became the nucleus of the tiny community, but it was also the biggest obstacle in the way of a new canal. The state legislature had approved construction in 1839. The right-of-way, however, extended through Fort Brady property, and the War Department refused consent to the project. When contractors showed up to begin work anyhow, they were driven off by soldiers. That ended that project.

The situation changed rapidly in the next decade. With the opening of the iron mines near Negaunee, shipping jam-ups at the Soo portage became routine. Ships were hauled around the falls on rollers and sledges, a few painful feet every day. Others had their cargo unloaded and carried to other ships on the far side of the falls. Ore piled up around the mineshafts as traffic backed up. The turning point came late in 1851. A sale of public lands attracted a large group of nationally prominent men to the Soo, and they saw for themselves the congestion there. Later generations would employ public relations specialists to set up similar displays in the national news media to mobilize public opinion; the principle worked just as well in 1851. Pressure finally resulted in action from Congress. A right-of-way through the fort was approved and 750,000 acres of public land set aside for payment to the construction company.

Work began in June, 1853, with Charles T. Harvey as the superintendent. It was the start of a two-year ordeal for him and his men. The locks, gates, and depth were the biggest ever assayed for an American canal. A mile-long channel had to be blasted from the rock. Stone for the lock walls had to be shipped from Marblehead, Ohio, and Walden, Ontario. Nineteen thousand tons of iron and 8,000 feet of timber were needed for the gates. Cholera killed 200 workers. Work went on right through the winter despite sub-zero temperatures and driving snow. When laborers went on strike over working conditions, Harvey closed the cookhouse to starve them back to the job. In two years and two weeks, it was done. On June 18, 1855, the brigantine *Illinois* passed successfully through the locks and the Soo was in business.

Meanwhile, across the river, the Canadian Soo was also growing. The Hudson's Bay Company continued to operate a trading post there until 1861. But it was mineral wealth that swelled the city. Copper was discovered at nearby Bruce Mines in 1846, and the Soo became a processing point. Francis Clergue established a pulp and paper mill and eventually became involved in iron mining in the Michipicoten area. By 1900 he had organized the Algoma Steel Company, the area's largest employer. There is just one lock on the Canadian side of the river, as compared to four on the American bank, but the Canadian Soo is five times the size of its U.S. counterpart, and is the economic hub of an enormous region rich in natural resources and beauty.

The Canal

There are locks on both sides of the international boundary at Sault Ste. Marie. But while the canal dominates the life of the Michigan city, it is almost a side attraction in Canada. There are four locks on the American side, all of them larger and newer than the lone Ontario facility. A panoply of tourist attractions surrounds the canal area in Michigan; in Canada, the lock is well away from the central part of the city, tucked behind the huge Abitibi Paper Company plant.

The Canadian Soo is a far more diversified place. It is a rail and industrial center; the major economic force in town is the Algoma Steel Company, second biggest in the country. The lock was built as something of an afterthought. In 1870 Canada was denied permission to send troops through the Michigan canal to put down the Riel Rebellion in Manitoba. (There was a good deal of American sympathy for the rebels, stimulated by the ever-present hope of annexation.) The Canadians managed to disperse the Riel dissidents but pondered the effects of a more serious threat sometime in the future. Accordingly, plans were begun for construction of a Canadian lock. It opened in 1895.

In the Michigan Soo everything is centered around the locks. It wasn't always that way. Support for the original canal in 1855 was far from unanimous. A sizable number of Soo residents made their living servicing the portage trade, and they wondered how they would survive when the canal ended that stopover traffic. There was no need to worry. Servicing the tourist trade now is a bigger business than the portage commerce ever was.

There are four ways to see the Soo Canal: (1) an overview at the Tower of History; (2) a close-up at the Army Corps of Engineers Information Center in Government Park beside the locks; (3) a leisurely land-based examination aboard the Tour Trains on a one-hour, fourteen-mile circuit of both the American and Canadian cities; and (4) best of all, a cruise through the locks. There are five boats on the American side and two on the Canadian making the trip, and all essentially cover the same route. So it comes down to a choice of the most convenient time and location for you. The American cruises are scheduled more frequently and over a longer season, but the Canadian boats are generally less crowded during peak times.

The Tower of History
This 210-foot-high shaft is, for good or ill, the most distinctive feature of the American Soo skyline. Situated just east of the locks, at 326 East Portage Avenue, the tower looms over some of the Soo's most historic ground. Fr. Jacques Marquette's chapel was on the approximate site, and one block nearer the river stands the house built by pioneer trader John Johnston. A small museum on the ground floor of the tower and a short film presentation provide an adequate historical perspective on the area. Then elevators take you up for a twenty-mile view, extending to the Canadian highlands and the mouth of Lake Superior. It is a unique perspective, enabling visitors to get their geographic bearings straightened away. The Tower is open daily, mid-May to mid-October. Hours are 9:00 to 9:00 in July and August, 9:00 to 5:00 at other times. There is an admission charge.

The Information Center
The area paralleling the American lock system has been turned into parkland with gardens, fountains, and observation points. Government Park extends far to the east, along the grounds of old Fort Brady. The Information Center is in the section adjacent to the locks. It contains exhibits about the locks that run from simplified to technical. A working model of a lock and a short introductory film help make it all comprehensible—almost. Also on display are photographs detailing the construction of the four locks. The center is open daily, mid-May to mid-November, 8:00 A.M. to 9:00 P.M. There is no admission charge.

The Soo Locks Tour Train
Directly across Portage Avenue from the Information Center is the depot for the Tour Train. A motorized tandem, the train runs past the locks and the historic buildings along Water Street, then across the International Bridge for a view from on high and a look at the Canadian lock. There is nothing on the tour that you can't do yourself by car or on foot. But it does relieve you from

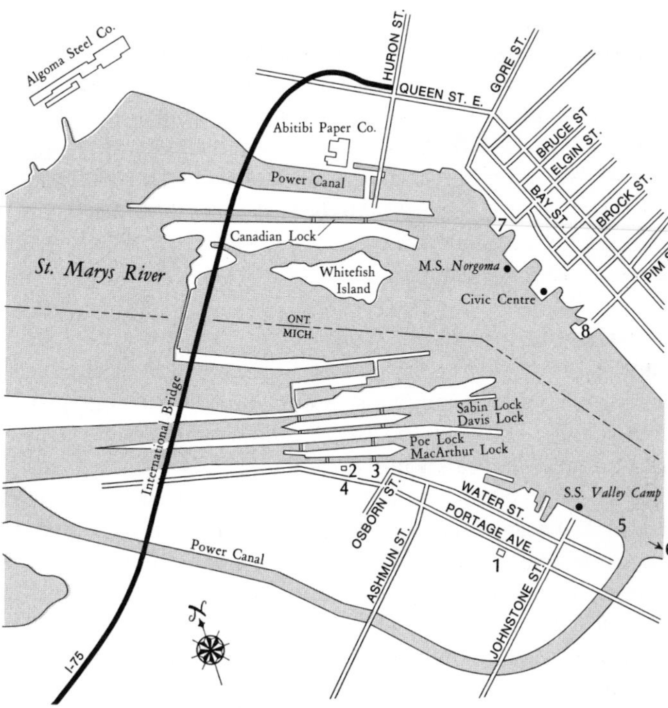

Algoma Steel Co.

HURON ST.

QUEEN ST. E.

GORE ST.

Abitibi Paper Co.

BRUCE ST

ELGIN ST.

BAY ST.

BROCK ST.

Power Canal

Canadian Lock

7

PIM ST.

St. Marys River

Whitefish Island

M.S. *Norgoma*

Civic Centre

ONT.
MICH.

8

Sabin Lock
Davis Lock

Poe Lock
MacArthur Lock

International Bridge

2 3

4

OSBORN ST.

WATER ST.

PORTAGE AVE.

ASHMUN ST.

S.S. *Valley Camp*

5

6

1

Power Canal

JOHNSTONE ST.

I-75

1 Tower of History
2 Information Center
3 Government Park
4 Soo Locks Tour Train
5 Locks Cruises, Dock 1
6 Locks Cruises, Dock 2
7 *Bon Soo* Dock
8 *Chief Shingwauk* Dock

The Soo Canal

the tedium of parking and coping with traffic, and you are able to concentrate on the scenery instead of the road while crossing the bridge. It is a fairly commercial operation, though, and features plugs for Portage Avenue souvenir stands that one may find annoying. The train runs daily from Memorial Day weekend to mid-October. Hours are 9:00 to 8:30, July to Labor Day; 9:00 to 7:30, last two weekends in June; and 9:00 to 5:00 in the other months. There is a charge.

The Locks Cruises
If time is short, this is the one Soo tour to take. Nothing compares with a trip through the locks yourself for getting a feel for the canal (which, by the way, is officially named the St. Marys Falls Canal). The canal has operated continuously on this site since 1855, but today's version looks nothing like the original. Since 1919 there have been four locks here, and each was built wider and deeper than the last. As the freighters get bigger the locks must keep pace; the canal's history is one of a continuing effort to stay even with increased traffic and shipbuilding technology. Two months after the opening, the two-masted brig *Columbia* became the first ore carrier to pass through the lock. Compared to today's ships it would look like a toy, just as vessels that were considered huge in the 1960s are dwarfed by today's super-freighters. The shape of the Lakes freighters gradually evolved through the late nineteenth century. The "lakers" were invented to carry bulk cargoes of ore and grain measuring in the thousands of tons. Their elongated, flat-bottomed shape is unique, immediately recognizable from Duluth to Montreal as the signature of Great Lakes shipping.

By 1870 the first State Lock had been outmoded. (This first lock had actually consisted of two 350-foot locks in tandem, with a width of 70 feet and a depth of 11.5 feet.) Gen. Orlando M. Poe, head of the Detroit office of the Army Corps of Engineers, was put in charge of building a second lock. This would be a single unit, 515 feet long, 80 feet wide, and 16 feet deep, built to the south of the State Lock. As work went on, it became apparent that the expense of the expanded canal was going to outstrip the state's ability to pay. Ownership of the locks was transferred to the Corps of Engineers in 1881 and the toll, which had been set at three cents a ton, was forever abolished. Three months later, the second, or Weitzel Lock, was opened. Even before it carried its first ship, though, it was outmoded. The ships were growing too quickly—in size and in number. By 1887 work had to begin on expansion of the old State Lock. Renamed the Poe Lock at its opening nine years later, it was 800 feet long, 100 feet wide, and 22 feet in depth. Critics complained that its dimensions were preposterous, unwarranted by the size of existing ships, and that the planners had overreacted. It was indeed the largest lock in the world. But by 1906, traffic on the canal exceeded the 50 million ton mark. The Poe was called on to handle 86 percent of that tonnage because the Weitzel Lock was not capable of taking the newer, larger ships. Again a replacement was needed. Col. Charles E. L. B. Davis of the Corps drew up the new plan. Instead of replacing the Weitzel, he proposed building a third, entirely separate lock north of the existing canal, with room provided for a fourth lock north of that.

These two locks are still in operation. The Davis, the third one from shore, opened in 1914; the Sabin, named for Davis's assistant, went into operation five years later. These locks are twins, and at 1,350 feet they remain the longest in the canal system. They were 550 feet longer than the Poe Lock which had been derided for excess when it opened only eighteen years before. At 80 feet in width they were slightly narrower than the Poe, but a shade deeper at 23.1 feet.

The new locks generated increased traffic, and the pressure to expand was inexorable. By the end of World War I the canal was carrying 76 million tons a year, and as a new world conflict approached, the canal was regarded as a vital element in national defense. Work began on a replacement for the antiquated Weitzel Lock to insure an uninterrupted flow of raw material to the war plants on the southern Lakes. In 1943, with troops stationed at the Soo to guard against sabotage, the MacArthur Lock opened. It is the smallest of the locks at 800 feet in length, 80 in width, and 31 in depth; in the postwar economic boom, this setup again proved unequal to the traffic. A record 128 million tons passed through the Soo in 1953. Gigantic new freighters, bigger than the existing locks could handle, were on the drawing boards. The result was the New Poe Lock, opened in 1968. At 110 feet in width and 32 feet in depth it is the largest in those dimensions in the canal, although 150 feet shorter than the Davis and Sabin locks. As it is, though, it is barely large enough for the 105-foot-wide, 1,000-foot-long behemoths that were launched in the 1970s, beginning with the *Stuart Cort*. Two-thirds of the iron produced in the United States and Canada passes through these locks on the giant freighters.

The locks cruise ships pass through one of the canals, then proceed up the river past the railroad and highway bridges. They cross over to the Canadian side for close-up views of Algoma Steel and the Abitibi Paper Mill. They then enter the Canadian lock, which is still a sizable facility at 900 feet in length, but of use only to shallow draft ships since it has a depth of only 16.8 feet. After running alongside the new riverfront developments of the Canadian city, the boats swing back across the river for a look at the quarter-mile-long Edison Hydroelectric Power Plant, built of stone blasted during the building of the canal. A power canal serving this plant completely encircles the downtown portion of the American Soo.

Cruises leave from two locations on the American side. Dock Number Two, closer to the locks, is at 500 East Portage Avenue, while Dock Number One is located at 1157 East Portage. From July to Labor Day there are twelve trips daily, starting at 8:00 A.M. from Dock One and twenty minutes later from Dock Two. The last boat leaves at 6:00 P.M. at Dock One, 5:40 P.M. from Dock Two. In late May and June boats leave from Dock One starting at 9:00 A.M.; in September to mid-October from Dock Two starting at 9:00. There is a charge. On the Canadian side, cruises generally run from June 1 to mid-October. Hours vary, and it is best to check locally for exact times. The *Chief Shingwauk* leaves from the Norgoma Dock near the foot of Pim Street. The *Bon Soo* leaves from the Holiday Inn dock, a few blocks to the west behind the Station Mall Plaza.

Tahquamenon Falls State Park

The wilderness has been pushed back to a comfortable distance at Tahquamenon Falls. Good roads lead to within half a mile of the upper falls. The morning newspapers from Detroit are on sale in stands at the parking lot. Half a million people come each year to walk through the forest and view the waterfall. But wander just a tiny bit off Michigan Highway 123, the road that leads from Paradise south to the falls, and you will find yourself once more in wilderness so vast and still that parking lots and morning papers seem like intrusions from a different planet. Tahquamenon has become so accessible that it is difficult to believe that as recently as 1943 there were no roads at all in this area, except for old logging tracks. Highway 123 was built as a Civilian Conservation Corps (CCC) project, a stimulus for the still nascent tourist industry in Michigan's Upper Peninsula. The CCC also was responsible for developing the nearby Seney National Wildlife Refuge (see chap. 6); so there was some good that came out of the Depression, at least for the U.P. These developments, however, remain only tiny slivers in the vast empty space that makes up this corner of Michigan's Upper Peninsula.

The Tahquamenon River plays a featured role in Henry Wadsworth Longfellow's *Song of Hiawatha*. To suit his ear, the New England poet altered many of the tribal place names in Michigan, supplied to him by Indian folklorist Henry Schoolcraft. The river, which Indian historians believe means "Marsh of the Blueberries," was rendered as "Tahquamenaw" in the epic poem. Hiawatha's friend, Kwasind, cleared the river of debris, then lost his life in its waters to a race of malevolent otters. Hiawatha built his canoe by its side. In reality, the river was an important element in the life of local tribes. They built camps on its shores, fished its waters and trapped along its banks. Later, near the end of the nineteenth century, lumbermen turned it into one of Michigan's great logging streams.

The river runs for ninety-four miles, rising in a series of springs in western Luce County and emptying into Lake Superior just south of Paradise. About three-quarters of the way through its run, the Tahquamenon tumbles over a 50-foot precipice at the head of a 200-foot-wide canyon. This upper falls resembles a small Niagara in terms of breadth and volume. In the eastern United States it is, in fact, exceeded only by Niagara in those dimensions. The Upper Peninsula, with its hilly terrain and rivers rushing to the lakes, is studded with waterfalls. More than 150 of them have been charted, mostly in the peninsula's western half, but none can touch Tahquamenon in majesty. The river goes on for another four miles from the upper falls, then tumbles down a series of lovely cascades to form the lower falls.

The river is known for the amber color of its water. The source of the color is neither mud nor downstream pollution. It comes from the tannic acid in the swamps drained by the river. Even in the previous century, it was referred to as the "golden river."

The Tahquamenon Falls State Park, which with 22,000 acres is the second largest in the Michigan system, has three units. They are the upper falls, the lower falls, and the river mouth. Except for a few miles, all three segments are connected by the river between the upper falls and the lake. Easiest access to all of them is by Highway 123.

The upper falls is the westernmost unit. Part of the attraction here is the walk to the falls through a magnificent forest of hemlock, maple, and birch. If you're lucky and arrive early in the morning or out of season and avoid the crowds, the quarter-mile stroll through this forest is reward enough for the trip. Even at midday the overhead growth is so thick that only thin shafts of sunlight penetrate to the forest floor. Around the falls is a 300-year-old section of a beech and maple climax forest, one of the few remaining in existence. This area is a laboratory for botanists who come here from all over the country to observe plant life that can be found in only a handful of places. The path forks near the top of the gorge; to the right a short continuation leads to the top of the falls. The roar of this torrent has been dimly audible, almost as a white noise, for most of the walk. Now it becomes overwhelming. During spring and early summer, 50,000 gallons of water a second plunge over these rocks. The view down the gorge indicates how far these 8,000-year-old falls have eroded upstream because of their tremendous cutting power against the underlying sandstone.

Back at the fork of the path, a left turn leads to a flight of stairs that descends to the bottom of the cliff for a close-up view of the upper falls' base. For the energetic, a footpath continues along the river all the way to the lower falls. It is a four-hour walk, according to park officials, and if you're up to the hike, it is well worth the effort. It winds past rapids and swirling pools in a lightly traveled portion of the river; chances of viewing wildlife are excellent. If you prefer driving, Highway 123 will take you to within a few hundred feet of these falls. Rowboats may be rented to reach the island lying between the cascades. The river drops a total of twenty-three feet over several short steps on either side of the island. There are 183 campsites at the falls unit, with an

Fifty thousand gallons of water a second plunge over Tahquamenon Falls in Michigan's Upper Peninsula. *Courtesy the* Detroit News.

additional 90 at the river mouth. The latter location is also noted for excellent fishing and a relatively insect-free setting.

Two excursion companies offer combination rail and boat trips to the upper falls. The Toonerville Trolley leaves from Soo Junction, just west of the Luce County line to the north of State Highway 28. The Tom Sawyer Riverboat trips begin at Slater's Landing, twelve miles north of Highway 28 near the town of Hulbert.

In the days before the road was cleared, the Toonerville line was the only way tourists could get to the falls—unless they wanted to backpack in. It has operated since 1927 under the same family ownership. The trips feature a six-mile jaunt aboard a narrow-gauge railroad car to Hunter's Mill, a former lumber camp. Travelers then switch to a riverboat and continue the journey downstream. The dock is located about a half mile from the falls. The trip takes from six and a half to seven hours. There are two trips daily on Monday through Friday in July and August, leaving Soo Junction at 10:00 A.M. and noon. In June, September, the first week of October, and all weekends, there is one trip at 10:30 A.M.

The Tom Sawyer Riverboat involves a one-and-a-half-mile train ride and a boat trip that enters the river further upstream than its competitor. A round trip lasts about three hours less than on the Trolley, which is an advantage if you're pressed for time. But the Tom Sawyer jaunt involves a longer automobile drive. The trips are priced at the same level. The Tom Sawyer Riverboat runs two daily trips, at 9:30 A.M. and 2:00 P.M., from July 1 to Labor Day. There is a single 10:30 A.M. trip the last two weeks in June and from Labor Day to mid-October. From Memorial Day to the second week in June it operates only on weekends at 10:30. Neither trip permits a visit to the lower falls, and the stopover at the upper falls is limited.

The Algoma Central

The Algoma Central Railway was not built for the tourist trade. It took fifteen years to lay its track across forest, rivers, canyons, and mountains, through an area that is still mostly wilderness. Its no-nonsense function was the transport of iron ore and lumber from the vast Algoma hinterlands to the mills of Sault Ste. Marie and the docks of Michipicoten Harbour. The process continues three-quarters of a century later; for the most part it is still cars loaded with ore and timber that ride this line. The railroad was a project of Francis Clergue, the founder of Algoma Steel, Ltd., and its aim was the exploitation of the country's rich resources. Clergue incorporated the railroad in 1899, but not until 1914 was it completed to Hearst, the junction with the Canadian National line, 296 miles to the north.

The tourists came later, after rail travel became a novelty and an exercise in nostalgia. Now the rugged Laurentian Highlands that were such a formidable barrier to the builders of the railroad form the setting for a trip that is among the most scenic on the continent. Travelers may go all the way to Hearst and spend the night before heading back to the Soo. But most riders prefer to take the day trip to Agawa Canyon, a beauty spot that looks like a smaller Yosemite. The train stops there for two hours, then turns around for the 114-mile return trip to the Soo. The entire journey lasts about nine hours, departing at 8:00 and returning at 5:00.

For the better part of its existence, until 1965, the railroad's official name was the Algoma Central and Hudson Bay. Supposedly, its initials (ACHB) stood for All Curves and High Bridges. That won't seem like an exaggeration on this ride. Passengers always seem to be looking out the window at the back half of the train as it lags behind on one sweeping curve after another. For the first thirty-two miles out of Sault Ste. Marie, the route climbs steadily, paralleling Highways 17 and 556 through comparatively well-settled country. But once past Searchmont, a lumbering town and ski resort, the journey enters a new dimension. From here on, there are no roads. What vehicles you see have been brought in by rail to serve a specific locality. Most transportation is by canoe or by foot. Backpackers and fishermen ride this train, too. They descend at tiny flag stations to be met by representatives of the lodges lying deep in the surrounding forest. The Algoma crosses 16,000 square miles of country just like this. For many wilderness lovers the railroad furnishes easy access to an area that is almost untouched—as soon as the train pulls out. There is exceptional fishing for speckled trout, walleye, and northern pike on nearly empty lakes. Moose hunters ride the Algoma in autumn and readily find success in these hills. Wilderness camping areas are plentiful. The railroad carries tents without charge, although canoes do count as excess baggage. Backpackers can get off at any stop and emerge whenever they choose at another flag stop down the line.

The Lake Superior road runs to the west, while far to the east is Route 129 to Chapleau. In between there is nothing but these tracks. Two and a half hours out of the Soo, the rails cross the Batchawana River and start to climb to 1,300 feet above sea level (the Soo sits at 600 feet). There are views into the river valley, but the most spectacular scenery is still to come. Twelve miles ahead is the Montreal River trestle, a 1,550-foot-long bridge built 230 feet above the ground. At the base of the trestle is a 100-foot-high dam, the power station from which the Canadian Soo draws most of its electricity. The view from either side of the passenger coach is splendid; the engine slows to a crawl so you can drink it all in.

For another ten miles the road continues to climb. At Milepost 102 it reaches 1,600 feet, the high point for the entire line. Then the bottom drops out. In the next twelve miles, the road drops 600 feet into Agawa Canyon. The scenery here exceeds everything that has gone before. Waterfalls tumble from towering rock walls to the canyon floor as the Agawa River flows swiftly past on its way to the Lake. For the first time Lake Superior becomes visible just beyond the treetops to the west.

There are two short walks to waterfalls that may be taken during the stopover at Agawa Canyon. A more strenuous trail leads to a lookout point on the canyon wall. The average walker can cover the distance in thirty-five minutes, according to the railroad. There is a large picnic area along the river, and box lunches are sold on the train for consumption amid this scenery.

The Algoma Central Railway runs north from Sault Ste. Marie into the Ontario interior. *Photo by Tom Buchkoe.*

There is also complete dining car service from departure until one hour before returning to the Soo. If you prefer, a more varied selection of box lunches is available in the Station Mall, a large enclosed shopping plaza built right behind the Algoma Central depot in the Soo. Two restaurants, Munchies and Guffins, are both open by 6:30 A.M. to provide food service for rail travelers.

The Agawa Canyon excursions operate daily from June to mid-October. There are no advance reservations, but tickets may be purchased the day before you want to travel. The railroad recommends that this be done. In peak season the trip frequently is sold out. Weekend crowds are especially heavy during the autumn color season, which runs from mid-September to the end of the schedule.

In the winter months, the Algoma Central becomes the Snow Train. The route covers the same areas as the regular tours, although the stopover is omitted at Agawa Canyon—the snow is simply piled too high there to permit picnics. The Snow Train operates from January to March on weekends only; advance reservations are essential. For times and reservation requests write Passenger Sales, Algoma Central Railway, Sault Ste. Marie, Ontario P6A 5P6. The phone number is 705-254-4331. Information on the overnight trips to Hearst may also be obtained at that number, as well as details on fishing and backpacking in the area.

Other Things to See

[1]   The lighthouse at Whitefish Point is the oldest on Lake Superior, dating from 1849 (although the existing tower was built later). The light is registered as a National Historic Site. The drive to the point along the shoreline is quite scenic; freighter-watchers will be rewarded by the sight of several ships beginning the difficult approach to the St. Marys Channel. The most famous Great Lakes disaster of recent years occurred off Whitefish Point in 1975 when, during a November gale, the freighter *Edmund Fitzgerald* was lost with twenty-nine hands.

[2]   Pioneer trader John Johnston's house was burned down by American raiders during the War of 1812 in retaliation for his British loyalty. By 1822 the family had built a new home on East Water Street in Sault Ste. Marie. This structure, standing on the site of the original Johnston home, is now the Chippewa County Historical Society Museum. The house is open daily, 11:00 to 5:00. There is no admission charge.

[3]   Adjoining the Johnston House is the S.S. *Valley Camp,* a recently retired Great Lakes freighter that is now a floating museum. Besides exemplifying the appearance of a contemporary ore boat, the *Valley Camp* also houses the Great Lakes Marine Hall of Fame. It is located at the end of East Water Street, by the hydroelectric power canal. Hours are 9:00 to 9:00, July to Labor Day; 9:00 to 6:00, mid-May and June. It is open daily. There is an admission charge.

[4]   Across the river is the Canadian Soo's own historic ship, the M.S. *Norgoma,* last passenger ship to operate on the Great Lakes. It ran from Owen Sound to the Soo until 1963 and has been a museum of local marine artifacts since 1974. It is now the centerpiece of the city's handsome new Civic Centre at the foot of Bruce Street. There is a six-story city administration building with a rooftop observation deck. Elsewhere in the area are recreational facilities and riverside walks with views across the rapids to the American locks and down the shore to the Canadian lock. Immediately to the west is the Station Mall. The ship is open daily, 10:00 to 6:00. There is an admission charge.

[5]   Charles Ermatinger was a fur trader, a pioneer settler of

the Canadian Soo. Like his counterpart across the river, John Johnston, Ermatinger prospered, married an Indian princess, and had his house burned down by the Americans in the War of 1812. But Ermatinger lived on the Canadian side of the border and, unlike Johnston, he and his house returned to prosperity after the war. His rebuilt home, at 831 Queen Street East, dating from 1814, is the oldest stone house in the country west of Toronto. It is now operated as a museum of the fur trade period. The house is open daily, 10:00 to 8:00, mid-June to Labor Day; 10:00 to 6:00 in May and early June and from Labor Day to mid-October. A donation is asked.

[6]   Sault Ste. Marie has two exceptionally fine parks within the city. Bellevue Park is a riverfront facility a few miles east of downtown on Queen Street. There are gardens, greenhouses, picnic facilities, great spots for freighter-watching, a small zoo, and a marine museum. The park is open all year, the museum from July to Labor Day. There is no admission charge. Up in the heights behind the Soo is Kinsmen Park, seven miles from downtown on Highway 17 and the park road. There are two waterfalls within its boundaries as well as a full assortment of recreational facilities.

[7]   Highway 17 becomes an exceptionally scenic road north of the Soo. It skirts Batchawana and Agawa bays, both rimmed by green hills, and seldom is far from the lakeside.

[8]   Lake Superior Provincial Park was established in 1944 to set aside a section of untouched shoreline as a natural preserve. Highway 17 runs right through the middle of the park, but most of the 600-square-mile area is inaccessible to all but boaters and hikers. The tract is dotted with small inland lakes, many of them lying just off the highway. As part of the effort to preserve a natural environment as fully as possible, none of them, except Sand Lake, permits motorboats. Highway 17 runs along the Lake Superior shoreline for about twenty miles. Along the way there are several scenic pullouts overlooking the water and the offshore islands, but most of the lakeshore at Gargantua Point is roadless.

[9]   Just north of the southern boundary of Lake Superior Provincial Park is Agawa Rock, an enormous outcropping above

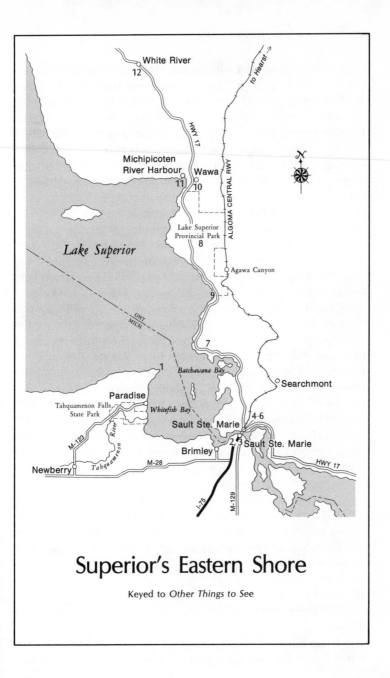

Superior's Eastern Shore

Keyed to *Other Things to See*

the lake that is covered with Indian pictographs rendered in red ocher paint. Scholars believe the paintings, dating from around 1600, were meant to depict a great, legendary battle in which the victorious party crossed the lake in canoes. The rock's spectacular setting and the ancient pictures combine to make this a moody, haunting place. The rock is reached by a short, mildly strenuous walk from the parking lot. There is no admission charge, but a pamphlet with a key to the paintings is on sale at automatic vending stands.

[10]   Wawa is supposedly the call of the wild goose, and there is a statue of that bird at the entrance to this town named after a birdcall. The cry that really made Wawa grow, however, was "Gold!" Starting in 1897, several mines were opened in the area. The Minto mine produced over one million dollars in gold and silver, and the Parkhill more than that. The mines are closed now, but a six-mile drive along an unpaved road will take you through the middle of the goldfields and past the ruins of the diggings. From Highway 17 south of Wawa, turn east on the road that continues west to Michipicoten River Village. The goldfield road turnoff goes to the north in three and a half miles. You emerge on Highway 101, on the south shore of Wawa Lake, just outside of town. The goldfield road carries only one-way traffic.

[11]   The Magpie River tumbles over a series of lovely waterfalls in the Wawa area. The high falls are the most spectacular; watch for the turnoff to the west just south of the entrance to town. Also worth seeing are the Silver Falls, just beyond Michipicoten River Village.

[12]   There's really not all that much to see in White River, although it is the center of an attractive resort area. It is in the record books, though, as the coldest spot in the land, chalking up a temperature of seventy-two degrees below zero, a mark that makes even Canadians shiver.

State and Provincial Parks on the Lake

Tahquamenon Falls State Park is described previously in this chapter.

There are two campgrounds near the lake in Hiawatha National Forest. Bayview Campground is on an isolated 2-acre site,

10 miles northwest of Raco, on Michigan Highway 28 and forest roads. There are 24 campsites, with swimming on a small Lake Superior beach. Monocle Lake Campground covers 23 acres on a small inland lake, 7 miles northwest of Brimley. There are 59 campsites.

Brimley State Park, 1 mile northeast of Brimley on Michigan Highway 221, occupies a scenic location at the southeastern corner of Whitefish Bay, looking across the mouth of the St. Marys to the wooded heights of Ontario. There is a small beach, full recreational facilities, and 270 campsites spread over 151 acres.

Batchawana Bay Provincial Park, 44 miles north of Sault Ste. Marie on Highway 17, is a small day-use park with 1 mile of beach and picnic facilities. There is no camping.

Pancake Bay Provincial Park, 50 miles north of Sault Ste. Marie on Highway 17, sprawls over 1,151 acres of rugged lake shoreline. There are full recreational facilities, hiking trails, fishing for rainbow trout, and 144 campsites.

There are three campgrounds scattered around Lake Superior Provincial Park. Agawa Bay, a 96-acre tract with 140 campsites, is the only one on Superior itself. It is located 5 miles north of the park boundary. On inland lakes are Crescent Lake, 1 mile inside the southern boundary, with 102 campsites; and Rabbit Blanket Lake, 40 miles north of the boundary, with 42 campsites. Access to the lake is also available at day-use facilities at Katherine Cove, 13 miles north of the boundary, and Old Woman Bay, 43 miles inside the park.

Obatanga Provincial Park, 21 miles southeast of White River on Highway 17, includes 22 inland lakes in a hilly, forested area. There is excellent canoeing and hiking and also a chance for bird watching. There are 124 campsites.

The days of the fur traders are recalled by Old Fort William, near Thunder Bay, Ontario. Courtesy Ontario Ministry of Tourism and Industry.

2

The Lakehead

The Canadian West begins at Thunder Bay. There is no ambiguity about it. You may argue about where the American West starts—the Mississippi River, the 100th meridian, or the Rocky Mountains—but there are no doubts about Canada. Lake Superior divides the country. You are still in the Province of Ontario on the western shore of the lake, but it is an Ontario far different from Toronto or Windsor or even Sault Ste. Marie. History and geography have combined to make this another region altogether.

For years, the split was a literal one as well. Until the 1880s and the completion of the Canadian Pacific Railway around the top of the lake, there was no overland connection between the eastern and western parts of Canada. Travel from one section to the other was accomplished either by lake steamer or by crossing into the United States. This was regarded, quite accurately, as a major hindrance to Canada's economic development. When British Columbia joined the new Confederation in 1871, a major condition was the construction of a transcontinental Canadian railroad. Not until 1885 was it completed above the lake, just six months before it reached the Pacific. An automobile road wasn't built around the lake until 1960. Even now the northern shore of

Lake Superior remains one of the least known, yet most beautiful, corners of the Great Lakes system.

The construction of the CPR is a great epic of Canadian and North American history. To the men who built it and unified a nation, the route around Lake Superior was one of the toughest tasks in the entire project. The sections across the empty plains of Manitoba and Saskatchewan and the mountain passes of Alberta and British Columbia were finished before the railroad had bested the rock and muskeg of the lakeshore. As chief engineer Sandford Fleming phlegmatically put it, "The area was not favorable for railroad construction." Fleming was, apparently, a master of understatement. One party searched for a prospective route north of Lake Nipigon and found nothing but black flies and mosquitoes. "We were no doubt the first human bipeds that had ever traversed this God-forsaken country—although perhaps we didn't fully realize the honour and glory of all this at the time," wrote a surveyor. Another surveying party found no great comfort along the lakeshore. "It was of the most barren and rugged description," they wrote, "traversed by high ranges of hills of primitive rock from which every vestige of vegetation had been removed by fire and quite impracticable for a railway."

The Grand Trunk Railway (which would become the Canadian National in the next century) had lost out to the CPR in the bid for the transcontinental contract. Now it tried to use its influence in Ottawa and the financial centers of Toronto and Montreal to block any route around the lake. It wanted the CPR limited to the west. The Grand Trunk suggested that the CPR tracks end at Pembina on the Manitoba-North Dakota border and that from there goods be shipped by American rails to Detroit where the Grand Trunk would pick them up. That way the Grand Trunk could retain its near monopoly on Ontario railroads.

The Lake Superior leg was, in truth, proving a financial drain on the CPR company. One troublesome mile took $700,000 to complete. Because of supply difficulties, dynamite factories had to be built on the spot to blast through the mountain ledges. Stone quarries were opened in the vicinity. Seven layers of track and three locomotives were swallowed up in one terrible bog. Even members of the CPR board of directors began to press for an

American route. This was hardly surprising; James J. Hill, who controlled the American line that would carry all the diverted traffic, sat on the CPR board. The route, however, had become a political and emotional issue. The American diversion was seen as negating the entire purpose of the railroad. The powerful influence of Prime Minister John A. MacDonald was thrown behind the Lake Superior leg, and the financial houses fell in line. In 1885 the second Riel Rebellion began in Saskatchewan, and troops from the east were carried to the scene aboard the CPR. That necessity cinched the case for the all-Canadian route.

Today the Trans-Canada Highway parallels the CPR tracks across this splendidly scenic country. A few twentieth-century lumbering towns break into the lakeshore at intervals, but for the most part the lake vistas are undisturbed and unforgettable. The area around Nipigon Bay, with its hundreds of offshore islands, would be difficult to match for sheer haunting beauty anywhere on the Lakes—or, for that matter, anywhere on the continent.

Old Fort William

At the end of the American Revolution, a number of unanswered questions were left hanging. It would take another war and another generation to settle them. No question was thornier than that of the boundary line between American and British territory west of Lake Superior. The wording of the peace treaty said it was fixed at "the customary canoe way." Exactly what this meant was open to debate. According to the British, it meant the St. Louis River, which flows into what is now Duluth harbor. The Americans begged to differ. They claimed the treaty referred to the Kaministikwia River, much further to the north. The debate went on for forty years and was not finally resolved until the Webster-Ashburton Treaty of 1842.

The long-range significance of the dispute was immense. It eventually preserved northern Minnesota and the wealth of the Mesabi iron range for the United States. At the end of the eighteenth century, though, no one was thinking of iron. The treasure then was fur. To the Montreal-based North West Company, the boundary dispute was of vital importance. Since 1768 its summer rendezvous had been held at Grand Portage, on the south bank of the Pigeon River, about forty miles south of the Kaministikwia. This was the place at which the trappers from the Rockies and the northern wilds would meet with company officers to exchange furs, accept payments, and plan strategy for the coming season. It was an annual July event and a focal point of the North West Company operations. By 1793 there were sixteen buildings at Grand Portage, and it was a major center for the fur trade. But John Jacob Astor's American Fur Company aggressively insisted it was situated on U.S. soil and demanded that it be taxed punitively. The North West Company decided the wiser course was to withdraw to the Kaministikwia and rebuild the rendezvous base there on grounds that were assuredly British. In 1803, Fort William, named for company director William McGillivray, held its first rendezvous.

The outpost has been restored as Old Fort William, the finest evocation of the fur trade era existing in North America. The restoration is about nine miles upstream of the site of the original, which is now lost within a tangle of railroad yards in the modern city of Thunder Bay. Within the confines of the old fort, the year remains 1816; it is always high summer for the North West Company. (In reality, the fort was seized that year by the rival Hudson's Bay Company and five years later was closed permanently as the two companies merged.) Each summer Old Fort William operates as closely to the original as historical research permits. Students from across Canada come here to take the parts of actual participants in the fort's history. Craftsmen go about the same duties they would have performed at the post a century and a half ago. Cooks tend ancient ovens to make bread. Voyageurs bring in their pelts, and Indians examine the trade goods at their encampment. A farm is worked to provide food for the settlement, and a doctor practices nineteenth-century medicine in the hospital. The Montreal partners, led by a bagpiper, tour the grounds on a daily round of inspection.

On the first Sunday of July, Old Fort William and all of Thunder Bay take part in the Great Rendezvous, a community-wide reenactment of the fur trade years. The revival is a somewhat more sedate version of the real thing, though. An original rendezvous was no place for the faint-hearted. It was the only contact the trappers had with civilization all year, and they were not about to miss any chance to let off steam and celebrate. They had something more than tea parties in mind, too.

Rendezvous time ends all too quickly, but there is much going on at the Fort William restoration at other times of the summer. Access to the fort is through an orientation center, where a short film places the fort in its historical setting. From there, visitors may either walk or take a horse-drawn cart to the gate of the fort itself. There are guided tours that leave approximately every fifteen minutes from the main gate, but it is just as easy to go around on your own. The costumed residents of the fort will answer any of your questions. On the main square there is a restaurant, the Cantine Salope, which serves appropriate dishes, such as freshly baked bread, stews, and soup.

The most imposing people you will see are the Montreal partners, or "pork-eaters," as the trappers called them scornfully. They were mostly Scots and insisted on dressing as if they had gone for a stroll in Montreal. In a wilderness where buckskin and moccasins were the style, a partner wore a dark suit, white shirt, frock coat, and a black beaver hat. In later years, he was carried in and out of the canoe by the crew and salutes were fired upon his arrival and departure. It all was meant to impart prestige and influence to these representatives of the home office, and it still makes a good show.

The events that ended Fort William's brief history began several hundred miles to the west in what is now Manitoba. The Earl of Selkirk, a major shareholder in the Hudson's Bay Company, was given an enormous land grant encompassing the basins of the Red and Assiniboia rivers to Lake Manitoba. The grant ran directly across major trade routes of the North West Company, and conflict was inevitable. The Montreal company stirred up the metis, the mixed French and Indian residents of the area, to harass Selkirk's colonists. In June, 1816, twenty of Selkirk's men, including the governor of the colony, were killed at Seven Oaks. Furious at the news, Selkirk marched on the base at Fort William one month later and seized it for Hudson's Bay. He appropriated its furs and supplies, then entered a long legal battle with the North West Company. The litigation drained the resources of both firms. Selkirk returned to England a broken man in 1818 and died two years later. The North West Company was nearly bankrupt. The court battle had eaten away its profits, and Selkirk's colony had nevertheless reestablished itself. The only solution was amalgamation, so in 1821 the two hated rivals combined and the post at Fort William closed for good.

Sixty years later the area revived with the coming of the Canadian Pacific Railway. But the fur trade was gone forever from Lake Superior, until recalled in another century at this restoration. Old Fort William is open daily, late May through September, 10:00 to 6:00. There is an admission charge. Signs on the Trans-Canada Highway south of Thunder Bay direct motorists to the fort with little difficulty.

Thunder Bay Harbor

The coming of the Canadian Pacific did more than link the head of Lake Superior to eastern Canada. The railroad also opened up the vast prairies of the west and turned the city at the lakehead into the largest grain-shipping port on the continent. In those days, however, there was no city at the lakehead. There were instead two medium-sized towns, Fort William and Port Arthur. The two merged in 1970 to form Thunder Bay, the largest city on the northern Great Lakes.

This is one city that must be seen from the water to be appreciated. Fortunately, that is easily arranged. Welcomeship, Ltd. offers sightseeing cruises of the harbor and the mouth of the Kaministikwia River. The harbor, ringed by its gigantic grain elevators, is one of the most distinctive on the Lakes. There are nineteen elevators in all, operated by cooperative pools from the prairie provinces. Their storage capacity is 100 million bushels of grain, the greatest concentration in the world. In one of them alone, Saskatchewan Pool 7, enough grain can be stored to make two loaves of bread for every person in North America. During the year, 445 million bushels of grain are shipped from this port.

The little sightseeing boats duck and bob around the huge grain carriers docked at the elevators to receive their loads. The focus of the harbor is the Keefer Terminal, a 180-acre facility that combines railroad yards, elevators, storage sheds, and docks. It was named after a Canadian family that was instrumental in promoting the St. Lawrence Seaway and turning Thunder Bay into a world port. Besides being commercially impressive, the harbor cruises also are quite scenic. Thunder Bay sits against a backdrop of green hills, topped by 1,600-foot Mt. McKay on the south. Directly across the bay is the Sibley Peninsula and the Sleeping Giant. The latter is a mountainous formation that resembles a man lying on his back. Almost seven miles in length, the formation is the subject of many legends involving enchanted spirits and lost silver mines. A mine is still there, on an island just off the southern end of the peninsula (see Other Things to See).

The site of Thunder Bay goes back to the beginning of exploration of the northern lakes. Fort William, or Thunder Bay

Southward as it became known after amalgamation, was a trading post as far back as 1678 when the French explorer Du Lhut landed there. The French put up a full-scale fort in 1717, but abandoned it during the wars with England later in the century. It was named Fort William by the North West Company when, in 1803, the firm moved its rendezvous there from Grand Portage, Minnesota. After North West's merger with the Hudson's Bay Company, though, the place became an obscure outpost. Soon the mouth of the Kaministikwia silted up, not to be cleared until the tracks of the CPR arrived in 1881. Port Arthur (or Thunder Bay Northward) began as a mining town in 1856, but gained importance in the 1870s as the start of the Dawson Road from the lake to Manitoba's Red River Settlement. It became a supply depot during construction of the CPR, and the first grain from the west rolled into town in 1883. Later on, however, the town and the railroad had a falling out, and the main CPR facilities moved to Fort William. A more diversified industrial base grew up in Fort William, while Port Arthur's economy remained tied to the shipment of grain.

The growth of Canada's vast wheat lands was made possible by two developments in the 1880s. The first, of course, was the extension of the CPR tracks and the accessibility they gave the once remote prairie to the markets of the east. The other was Red Fife, a breed of wheat developed by a young Ontario agronomist, David Fife. He had been experimenting with hard wheats that matured quickly, varieties suited to the short growing season of the northern prairies. A wandering cow almost devoured the entire crop, but Fife salvaged a few heads which provided the basis for the western wheatlands. New milling processes also had been developed, making hard wheat more marketable. The new wheat reduced the risk presented by early frosts, and settlers flooded onto the prairies—many of them coming up from the United States.

The wheat prospered, but the men who grew it were not doing as well. Farmers had no control over the marketing apparatus and felt they were caught in a squeeze between the railroad and the owners of the storage elevators. The breaking point came in 1897. The CPR directed that it would load no wheat that did not come from the elevators. To the farmers it appeared that the two middlemen were combining against them. Farmer agitation managed to get the order rescinded in 1900, and having once exerted their power, the farmers were far from through. They formed the Territorial Grain Growers Association in 1902 to pressure the federal government for marketing assistance. In a few years, cooperatives had formed to run their own elevators and sales organizations. Price controls on wheat had been adopted by the government during World War I, but were dropped afterward because of eastern political pressure. The farmers, seeing how easily prices could be managed, decided to operate their own control mechanism by forming the Wheat Pools, voluntary marketing associations, in 1924. The pools give the western grain-grower some control over the price of his crop, and it is their towering elevators that surround the harbor of Thunder Bay. Tours of these elevators are usually available in July and August. Inquire at the Tourist Office, 134 Arthur Street, Thunder Bay Northward.

Cruises of the harbor are conducted daily from June through September. The tours aboard the 200-passenger *Welcome* last two hours and depart at 1:45, 3:45 and 7:30. A fourth cruise up the river to Old Fort William leaves at 10:00 A.M. from mid-June to Labor Day. Cruises begin at the marina at the foot of Arthur Street, Thunder Bay Northward.

Ouimet Canyon Provincial Park

What went through Louis Hennepin's mind when he first looked at Niagara Falls? Or Étienne Brulé's as he roamed where no European ever had set foot before—what did he think as he gazed at Superior's "big sea water"? Those sensations are difficult, if not impossible, to recapture today in a world too full of tourism and empty of experience. Niagara is still an impressive sight, but so eroded by creeping trivialization that it takes a powerful imagination to see it with uncluttered vision. Even on Superior, largest and wildest of the Great Lakes, the tourist industry has managed to institutionalize the wilderness in all but a few places. Ouimet Canyon remains one of the few.

There is a sign on Highway 17, about forty-three miles east of Thunder Bay, pointing to a gravel road that runs north. The directional marker reads Ouimet Canyon Provincial Park. That is it—just the bare essentials. No billboards or souvenir stands; only an arrow pointing to a gravel road.

If you follow this road, it will twist and wind, proceeding deeper and deeper into nothing at all for about seven miles. Then as you are ready to give up and turn around, when you begin to believe this imaginary canyon is a practical joke dreamed up by the Ontario Ministry of Transportation to play on the unwary traveler, the road ends at a small parking area. If you are very lucky it will be empty. A pathway leads across a bridge and then through a forest. In about one-quarter of a mile the path branches. You take a few steps to the right and suddenly, there it is—350 feet deep and 500 feet across—a vast, two-mile long chasm in the earth.

There are no fences on the rim, no maps, no guides, nothing to intercede between the traveler and the wilderness. There is no sound, either, only the wind rushing through the trees on its trip from Lake Superior (visible above the branches to the east). This must be something close to what Brulé felt, three and a half centuries ago, when the entire land lay open and untouched. The only intruder from the twentieth century is yourself.

Ontario plans to keep the canyon this way as much as possi-

Ontario's Ouimet Canyon Provincial Park remains an uncluttered wilderness. *Courtesy Ontario Ministry of Tourism and Industry.*

ble. The park is under development. There are plans for a signed parkway rather than a gravel entrance road, wayside exhibits instead of an empty path, and a naturalist-ranger on duty at the rim. However, all intensive and noisy activities will be banned.

The canyon has been known since the first homesteaders moved into the region. It was named after a defunct station on the Canadian Pacific Railway, which was in turn named for Joseph Alderic Ouimet, a jurist and politician. There was trapping and lumbering activity in the canyon after 1885, and as recently as the 1960s some quantity of aspen and spruce were taken from it; but the incursions have been minor.

Ouimet Canyon was formed during the last Ice Age. Molten rock opened a deep crack in the sheet of igneous rock that composes the earth's surface there. Such activity was common in the area, and there are several other canyons nearby, but none with walls so sheer or with a floor so clear of debris. Geologists think Ouimet Canyon functioned as a channel carrying meltwaters away from the receding glaciers, and so was able to rid itself of any debris. Erosion by water and ice then shaped it.

Most of the rim is forest of trembling aspen and white cedar, among the loveliest of northern trees. On the canyon floor, however, are found plants of an even more northerly nature. Nowhere else in the world do several Arctic species grow this far south. The Arctic wintergreen, one such plant, grows here by the thousands. Some of the plants are relics of the Ice Age. They have survived here for more than 10,000 years because of the canyon's peculiar ecology. Depressions in the canyon ridges on the floor retain frigid air, emanating from accumulations of stagnant ice forever shielded from sunlight. The thick moss carpet and unhindered movement of air also contribute to turning this area into an isolated piece of the Arctic. Many plants, such as the pussy willow and white cedar, that normally grow upright are found in dwarfed or prostrated positions here because of the unusually harsh microclimate.

The traveler can walk along the rim for the entire length to several lookout points, each of them giving new perspectives on the gorge. Extreme caution is required, however, because of the lack of any safety railings, and it is advised that pets and small children be kept in hand. When the park development is finished there will be guided tours to the canyon floor, as well. For the present, though, there is only the silence of the rim. And that is well worth the trip.

Ouimet Canyon's peculiar ecology supports plants usually found only in Arctic regions. *Courtesy Ontario Ministry of Tourism and Industry.*

Other Things to See

[1]   Highway 17 between Marathon and Nipigon is one of the great scenic roads of North America. Roughly paralleling the course of the Canadian Pacific Railway, the highway winds high above the lakes, through a series of hills and rocky ridges, and opens out on the island-studded bays of Superior's northern shore. There are several scenic turnouts and picnic areas along the route. The most spectacular of them is Kama, between Rossport and Nipigon; it overlooks Nipigon Bay, the most northern point of the Great Lakes.

[2]   Most of the towns in this area are twentieth-century developments built around paper mills. They are bustling communities, but not terribly interesting for the traveler. An exception is Rossport. Set against a bay filled with hilly green islands, Rossport is a delightful hideway. A nineteenth-century hotel and restaurant, the Rossport Inn, adds to the ambience. There is also a marina at which boats can be chartered to pursue the plentiful lake trout in the area.

[3]   Amethyst is a purplish semiprecious gem (the name comes from a Greek word meaning "wine-colored") that occurs plentifully along Lake Superior's northwestern corner. The Thunder Bay Amethyst Mine is the largest yet discovered. It turned up during construction of a road to a forestry tower in 1967, and has since become the largest producer of amethyst in Ontario. A rough dirt road to the mine is marked on Highways 11 and 17, about midway between Nipigon and Thunder Bay. It's about five jolting miles from the highway to the mine, and there's only a 50 percent chance that a van can make the trip. Standard cars, though, usually have no problem. There are exhibits of amethyst there, and by paying a small fee you can get into the pit and scratch around for yourself. It is a rockhound's delight. The mine is open daily, dawn to dusk, May to November.

[4]   Even more precious than amethyst is silver, and there used to be plenty of that found around here, too. The vein was discovered at the southern tip of the Sibley Peninsula by copper prospectors in 1868. It was traced into the lake, to a small island just offshore. A combine headed by Maj. A. H. Sibley bought the

island from the Montreal Mining Company. The island was expanded to ten times its natural size to house machinery and buildings, and cribbing was placed around it to act as a breakwater. Over 1.7 million ounces of silver were taken from the island before the vein became too deep to exploit economically. The mine shut down in 1884, but the mainland mining village, Silver Islet, still remains as part of Sibley Provincial Park.

[5]   Centennial Park is an 847-acre slice of Thunder Bay that has been kept in an almost natural state. Located in the northeastern corner of the city, it has fine hiking trails, a restored lumber camp and museum (with lumberjack meals in the cookhouse), a narrow-gauge railroad that makes a circuit of the park, and skiing in winter. Take Black Bay Road from Highways 11B and 17B to reach the park. The lumber camp and railroad operate from June to Labor Day; the park itself is open daily all year. Exhibit hours are 10:00 to 10:00. There is no admission charge.

[6]   There are exhibits on Thunder Bay's colorful fur-trading, grain-shipping, and silver-mining past in the Historical Society Museum. It is located next to City Hall in the Southward, at 219 South May Street. The museum is open 11:00 to 5:00 daily, mid-June to mid-September; 1:00 to 5:00 Tuesday through Sunday, rest of the year. There is an admission charge.

[7]   There are two good viewing areas from which to take in the sweep of Thunder Bay. In the Northward it is Hillcrest Park, located on an escarpment above the downtown area on High Street. It looks out across the harbor to the Sleeping Giant. In the Southward, the views are quite a bit loftier. A toll road leads up to the 600-foot point on Mt. McKay and provides an interesting vantage point above the Kaministikwia River and its industrial installations as well as the surrounding forests. The road is a bit tricky to find, but if you can get to the James Street swing bridge on Highway 61B and turn east on City Road, it is well marked from there on.

[8]   Mt. McKay and the adjacent peaks are lively ski areas in winter. The Mount Norway and Candy Mountain ski areas are just southwest of the city on Highway 61. Mount Norway also features the Big Thunder ski jump, which at ninety meters in

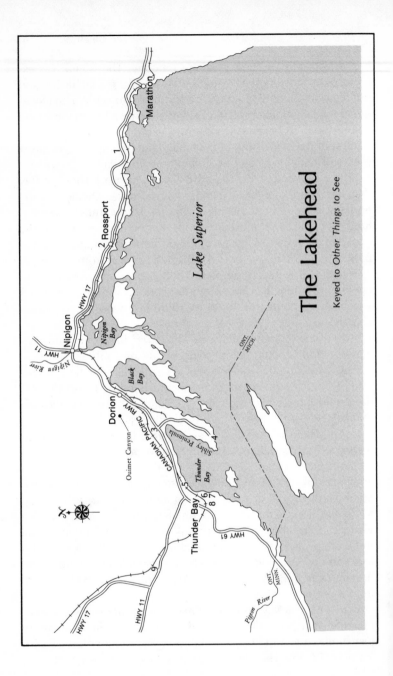

The Lakehead

Keyed to Other Things to See

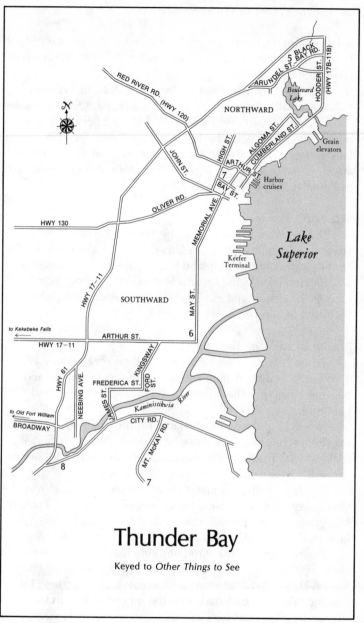

Thunder Bay

Keyed to *Other Things to See*

height shares the honor for world's highest with the Lahti jump in Finland. It is used as a training site for teams in international competitions.

[9]   There is a fascinating legend about the 128-foot-high Kakabeka Falls, just west of Thunder Bay. An Ojibwa maiden captured by Sioux raiders was forced to lead her captors to her home village. Instead, she led them right over the brink of the falls and quickly ended that particular invasion threat. The falls are now part of a provincial park. They are seventeen miles west of Thunder Bay on Highways 11 and 17.

Side Trip

The Nipigon River, one of the favorite canoe routes of the voyageurs, empties into Lake Superior from Lake Nipigon. The country surrounding this inland lake is a sportsman's dream, with walleye and trout in the streams and moose and bear in the hills. One of the better-equipped outposts is Jellico, forty-eight miles northeast of Nipigon on Highway 11.

Provincial Parks on the Lake

White Lake, 35 miles east of Marathon on Highway 17, is a 3,980-acre facility on an inland lake with sandy beaches and fine pickerel fishing. There are good walking trails and 300 campsites.

Neys, 15 miles west of Marathon on Highway 17, has an excellent sandy beach for those hardy enough to brave Superior's frigid waters. The fishing is also good, and there is a caribou herd in the 8,150-acre park. There are 120 campsites.

Rainbow Falls, 5 miles east of Rossport on Highway 17, encompasses both the big lake and inland Selim Lake. There are hiking trails along the Selim River and its waterfalls. The 1,422-acre facility has 207 campsites.

Sibley takes in the entire peninsula that seals off the eastern shore of Thunder Bay. The entrance is 20 miles east of Thunder Bay on Highway 17, and the park extends southward for 23 miles into the lake. The park makes up the rugged highlands that form the Sleeping Giant as well as the old silver mining town of Silver Islet (see Other Things to See). It has many recreational opportunities, ranging from swimming to cross-country skiing to moose-watching. There are 160 campsites.

Kakabeka Falls is described in Other Things to See. There are 100 campsites.

Middle Falls, 41 miles southwest of Thunder Bay on Highways 61 and 593, is a 2,000-acre park located on the Pigeon River (the international boundary between Ontario and Minnesota). There are fishing and picnicking facilities and a seven-mile hiking trail along the cascades of the Pigeon. There are 20 campsites.

Iron ore and grain are loaded aboard huge freighters in Superior's busy harbor. *Courtesy Wisconsin Division of Tourism.*

Duluth and the American Lakehead

To the rest of mid-nineteenth-century America, the Lake Superior country was inconceivably remote. Gold had been discovered in distant California and covered wagons plodded along the trail to Oregon, but even those Pacific outposts seemed near and accessible compared to the northern reaches of Michigan, Wisconsin, and Minnesota. To the pre-Civil War generation, a tour of duty in an Army post there was the equivalent of being stationed in Devil's Island to a Frenchman. In Congress, an appropriations bill for some internal improvement in the area was usually met with hilarity and disbelief. In the debate over the canal, Henry Clay said that the Soo was more remote than the moon. His fellow Kentuckian, Rep. J. Proctor Knott, improved on that in an 1871 oration that for a time made Duluth a national symbol of the wild and desolate northern frontier. The impetus to Knott's address was a request for funds to finance a railroad to the port of Duluth. In a classic outburst of nineteenth-century ridicule, Knott mused aloud about this railroad's terminus: "Duluth. The word fell upon my ear with peculiar and indescribable charm, like the gentle murmur of a low fountain stealing forth in the midst of roses. Duluth. 'Twas the name for which my soul panted for years. But where was Duluth?

Never in all my limited reading had my vision been gladdened by seeing the celestial word in print. Its dulcet syllables had never before ravished my delighted ear." Knott went on and on in this vein. The speech gained wide circulation in the press, and Duluth, which had been reduced to a near ghost town only six years before, became known across the country.

Within two more decades, though, Duluth would be a name familiar everywhere. Even as Knott spoke, enthusiastic citizens were digging across the top of Minnesota Point to create a canal into the city's harbor. Iron ore had been found at Lake Vermilion in the nearby hills. The Northern Pacific Railroad had arrived from St. Paul. Duluth had become a boomtown that even the panic of 1873 could only stagger, not destroy. It had completely absorbed the old fur trading post of Fond du Lac, the first settlement in the area, and was engaged in a heated economic rivalry with its sister city across the harbor, Superior, Wisconsin. By 1890, Duluth was a prosperous little city, but bigger ore finds in the Minnesota hinterland were about to transform it completely.

The lumbering industry had swept across Michigan like a locust swarm, swallowing up the state's vast stands of timber with an insatiable appetite. By the 1890s it was Minnesota's turn. A peak of 462 million board feet of lumber passed through the port of Duluth in 1899. In nine more years, the total was less than half of that; by 1919 it had fallen below 100 million board feet. Duluth's last significant year as a lumber port was 1924, but the industry had made several fortunes while it lasted.

A more permanent source of wealth was taking shape simultaneously. The Vermilion iron strike had touched off a mining rush. There had been vague pioneer reports and Indian legends of vast deposits of iron in the northern hills, and men from all over the country came to Minnesota to search for them. Among the searchers were the members of the Merritt family of Duluth. The father, Lewis H. Merritt, had joined the short-lived gold rush to Vermilion just after the Civil War. He found no gold but did see plentiful amounts of iron ore. He returned to Duluth without his fortune, but the iron stayed in his mind. As his four sons grew he told them what he had seen. The Merritts were employed as timber cruisers, roaming the hills to seek out likely stands of trees for the lumber industry. As they searched, they also began scanning the ground for traces of ore. In 1890, their diligence was rewarded. Near what was to become the town of Virginia, they found the Mountain Iron Mine—the first strike on the enormous Mesabi Range.

The Merritts were not miners, so they felt it best to hire an experienced iron man to lead the explorations for them. The problem was that no one with any mining knowledge believed what the Merritts were saying. Previous experience indicated that ore was found at considerable depth and that shafts had to be sunk to exploit it, while the Merritts insisted that the ore at the Mesabi was just below the surface; some of it could even be scooped out by hand. Their chosen expert, J. A. Nichols, was no less incredulous than the rest. Years later, Leonidas Merritt described their first visit to the site with Nichols: "If we had gotten mad and kicked the ground right where we stood we could have thrown out 64 percent ore, if we had kicked it hard enough to knock off the pine needles. But, of course, we did not have any idea that this ore could possibly be found, if found at all, except at considerable depths. We were influenced, more or less, by the traditions of the miners. Nichols said that he had something of a reputation as a mining man and that he did not propose to be called, with the rest of us, farmers." The dubious Nichols did obtain a sample that tested at 64 percent purity. The Merritts promptly took out 141 leases to mining rights in the area.

The Merritts developed the Duluth, Missabi, and Northern Railroad, linking their mines to Lake Superior. They attracted eastern capital to the project, and, with Pittsburgh money, the Oliver Iron Mining Company was formed to exploit the field. (The firm became one of the major elements in the 1901 formation of the United States Steel Corporation.) The wealth of the Mesabi eventually poured back into Duluth. The Merritts, however, were not experienced financiers, and this was an era of rapacious business practices. They entered into a financial arrangement with John D. Rockefeller, which was about as safe as sitting down to lunch with a leopard. Within a matter of years, the Merritts had lost their railroads, their mines, and most of their fortune. They lived on as embittered men in their hometown that they had enriched. A statue of Leonidas Merritt in miner's garb stands in front of the public library at Mountain Iron, one the few surviving tributes to the Mesabi's founding family. The mine itself closed down in 1956 after shipping out a total of 48 million tons of iron ore.

The Apostle Islands

The northern route to the Mississippi River had been discovered in 1680 by Daniel Greysolon, Sieur du Lhut, a French soldier and adventurer whose name would eventually be attached to the Minnesota city at the lakehead. The ancient Indian canoe trail, down the Brule and St. Croix rivers, made the northern Wisconsin coast an important French connection in the fur trade. The French had come to Chequamegon Bay, the hinge of this shoreline, as early as 1659. Pierre Radisson and Medart Chouart de Grosseilliers had trapped and spent the winter on the bay. Six years later, Fr. Jean Allouez became the first permanent European resident, establishing a mission among the Ottawa near the present city of Ashland. Repeated raids by the Sioux forced him to abandon it; a later attempt by Fr. Jacques Marquette also failed for the same reason. But the French were determined to establish a military presence on the bay, and in 1693 Pierre Le Sueur was dispatched to the area with that assignment. Le Sueur sized up the situation and decided an island post would be far easier to defend. This left him with quite a choice, since the bay is speckled with islands. Early explorers thought they counted twelve and so named them the Apostles. Actually, there are twenty-two islands in the group, but no one has seen fit to tamper with the original name. The Apostles are now a national lakeshore. The island Le Sueur chose for his post, Madeline, the largest of the group at 14,000 acres, remains in private hands. It is the most significant of the islands historically, though, and does contain a state park. It is also the most accessible, with frequent ferry service from Bayfield on the mainland. (Bayfield also is the departure point for boat tours through the Lakeshore.)

Le Sueur's outpost on Madeline was named La Pointe. It became the commercial hub of the western lakes for the next 150 years—but not without a few interruptions. It was moved a number of times and left deserted before final stability came on the eve of its economic collapse. The island had long been a center of Indian life before the French arrived. Archaeological evidence places prehistoric peoples on Madeline 3,000 years ago. It was the traditional homeland of the Chippewa. According to legend, though, the place was abandoned after a period of misrule and chaos culminated in cannibalism. Thus, when Le Sueur arrived the island was uninhabited.

La Pointe prospered for five years. If anything, it prospered too well. The market became glutted with French furs, and the traders' licenses were revoked. The official post was withdrawn, and for twenty years La Pointe functioned as a gathering place for illegal traders. But France soon lost the Hudson Bay area to England, and it became imperative to reopen the western Lake Superior line to the American interior. In 1718, Paul le Gardeur, Sieur de St. Pierre, led a detachment back to Madeline Island and built a new fort, also called La Pointe. He chose a location about two miles north of Le Sueur's post, on the island's western shore rather than the south. The area now adjoins the island's marina.

The French maintained the operation until 1762, when it fell to England during the French and Indian Wars. Three years later, the British came in and burned the deserted buildings. The location was too valuable to ignore, however, and Mackinac traders Alexander Henry and Jean Baptiste Cadotte returned to the ruins and started up the traffic in furs once more. There were no more permanent settlers, though, until 1793 when Cadotte's son Michel became the island's first fulltime resident. An officer of the North West Company, the Montreal firm that his father's partner had helped found, Cadotte moved La Pointe back to its original position on the south shore and settled in for a forty-four-year stay. The island became American territory, but Cadotte simply switched his citizenship and remained. The American Fur Company took over the fur trade. Cadotte went to work for them and cheerfully married off his daughters to the Yankee traders who accompanied the new firm.

As the fur trade began winding down on the Great Lakes, the company saw the possibilities for another trading boom— whitefish, a Great Lakes delicacy that was coming into favor in the East. The La Pointe harbor was not big enough to accommodate a fishing fleet, so in 1835 the town was moved again. This time it ended up in its present location, about three miles north of Cadotte's village. In the next seven years, La Pointe enjoyed the

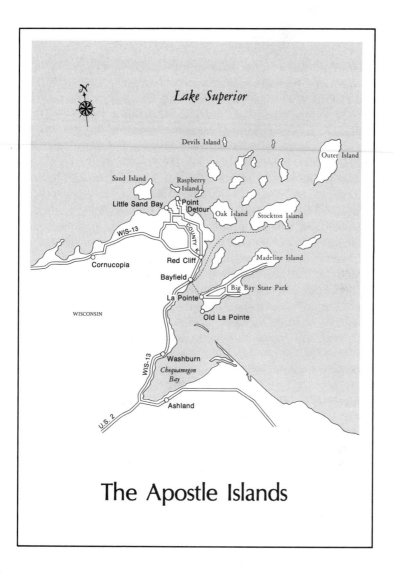

The Apostle Islands

greatest prosperity it had ever known. The company fishing fleet thrived, and a small traffic continued in furs.

A Protestant missionary, Rev. Sherman Hall, had arrived in 1830. He made the island his base for the next twenty years. In 1835 Fr. Frederic Baraga came to establish the permanent Catholic mission that had eluded Allouez and Marquette two hundred years before. Baraga, born in Yugoslavia of minor Austrian nobility, was a dynamic religious figure on the northern frontier. He had entered holy orders after receiving a law degree. Fascinated by the American Indians, he requested an assignment on the Great Lakes. He remained at La Pointe for nine years, building St. Joseph's Church and gathering European artwork for its interior. Baraga traveled the remote Lake Superior shoreline in winter and became known as the "snowshoe priest." He wrote of his experiences in books that became European best-sellers and established an early cult of the Indian there. Baraga built a new mission in L'Anse, Michigan, in 1843 and moved there the next year. Eventually, he would become the North's first bishop.

Meanwhile, the American Fur Company was running into transport problems with its fish. In 1842, shockingly, the mighty company went bankrupt. With its major employer gone, La Pointe lost its economic importance and became a backwater. Since the 1890s, though, it has steadily grown as a summer resort, especially popular among Minnesotans. It is now undergoing a major condominium resort development with a conference center and the obligatory Robert Trent Jones golf course.

A historical museum occupies the site of the American Fur Company post. Its main building was actually part of the company operation. The museum also incorporates the old town jail, a pioneer barn, and a cabin that stood on the island as a refuge for shipwreck victims. Exhibits deal with pioneer days on the island and the various La Pointes, with especially interesting artifacts from the original missions of the Reverend Mr. Hall and Father Baraga. The museum is open daily, mid-June to mid-September, 10:00 to 5:00. There is an admission charge.

The museum is a two-block walk up from the ferry dock. At the dock itself is the post office. The building dates from 1830

The Madeline Island Museum in Wisconsin's Apostle Islands preserves the trading post of Pierre LeSueur. *Courtesy Wisconsin Division of Tourism.*

and was originally part of the Protestant mission. It was moved here from another location. A right turn from the dock leads into La Pointe's business district, such as it is. It consists of a few shops and cottages and a pair of old churches. St. Joseph's stands on the same spot as Father Baraga's church, although the present structure dates from 1909. Continue through the town and around the marina to a site marked by a large white cross. This is the old Indian cemetery and the location of the island's first Catholic mission. Just beyond it is the location of the second La Pointe, founded by St. Pierre in 1718. Several ruins of that outpost remain. If you've brought a bike or car, you can continue on to the remains of the La Pointe of Le Sueur and Cadotte, and then go on a complete circle tour of the island and its state park. If you're on foot and just visiting for the day, the walk to the cemetery is about as much as can be comfortably handled. It's a two-mile round trip from the dock and back.

Ferries leave Bayfield for the fifteen-minute crossing to Madeline Island twenty-six times a day from late June to Labor Day. There is less frequent service at other times of year. Before mid-May and after the second weekend in October, there are only eight daily trips. Reservations are not accepted.

The Apostle Islands sightseeing cruises also leave from the Bayfield dock. A variety of trips, varying in route and length, are offered daily. The first one leaves at 10:00 A.M. A five-and-a-half-hour daily voyage swings around the lighthouse at Devils Island, stopping for a picnic lunch en route. Check locally for schedule and prices with the Apostle Islands Cruise Service. The phone number is 715-779-3925. Reservations are advised for these cruises during the peak summer season.

The cruise line also operates a shuttle boat between Bayfield and Stockton Island, the best-developed island in the National Lakeshore. There are two campgrounds on the island, along with hiking trails and a ranger station. Nature walks led by a ranger and evening interpretive programs are also offered there.

Park information offices operate in Bayfield and at Little Sand Bay, twelve miles northwest by paved road. The Little Sand Bay office has exhibits relating to the National Lakeshore and also schedules shuttles to many of the smaller islands. Short excursion cruises to Raspberry and Sand islands run from Little Sand Bay; private boats may be rented in Bayfield for those wishing to explore on their own. There are no overnight accommodations (except those for campers) on any of the Lakeshore islands, and no restaurants.

Sailing is one way to observe the beauty of the Apostle Islands. *Courtesy Wisconsin Division of Tourism.*

Minnesota Point

The western edge of Lake Superior is a place of rare and arresting beauty. Towering cliffs, part of the rock bowl that surrounds Superior, rise from the water to mark the limits of the Great Lakes system. For a length of thirty miles, the city of Duluth squeezes onto the narrow shelf between the water and the 800-foot-high escarpment. Streets and homes climb the side of this barrier wall and look down upon the business district and harbor. It is one of the most striking settings of any city in the country.

Duluth began on the less exciting foundation of a nine-mile-long sandbar. This narrow appendage to the mainland, Minnesota Point, is the longest freshwater sandbar in North America. As it extends into the lake, it almost meets another long bar reaching out from the opposite shore and called, fairly enough, Wisconsin Point. The gap between the two bars is the natural entrance to the harbor of Duluth and its sister port, Superior, Wisconsin.

Minnesota Point figured in local history even before Europeans arrived here. The Chippewas took note of the bar's impressive length and concluded it had been formed by supernatural means. A young brave, they said, had been trapped on the south shore. Surrounded by the Sioux, with the lake at his back, the Chippewa prepared himself for death. But the Great Spirit formed a land bridge for him across the water, and as he fled the bar sank behind him into the lake, cutting off pursuit. So there is a little touch of the Biblical Red Sea in Lake Superior.

Daniel Greysolon mentioned the Point when recounting his expedition to the area in 1679. He gathered warring Sioux and Chippewa there and attempted to make peace. The French soldier and explorer was aware that a fortune in fur lay in the Minnesota hinterland, but it would be impossible to exploit unless there was peace among the tribes. His attempts did not meet with lasting success. Greysolon, whose aristocratic title was the Sieur du Lhut, did manage to get the city named after himself, however, although it took two more centuries to accomplish that.

Starting in 1752, the Point was a base for wintering houses built by fur traders, but not for 101 more years was there a permanent settlement there. In 1852, George R. Stuntz was sent by the United States surveyor-general's office to take a look at the western lakehead. Stuntz was a mineralogist as well as a surveyor, and he liked what he saw. Not only did Minnesota Point and the mouth of the St. Louis River provide a natural harbor, but there was evidence of valuable mineral deposits in the hills nearby. Stuntz returned the next year and settled down on the Point, putting up a dock, a house, and a trading post. In 1856, a village was platted on the Point and the area began to grow. Several of the new residents, eager for a suitable name to bestow on the town, made a deal with a missionary in neighboring Wisconsin. Rev. Joseph G. Wilson would be given two lots in the new city in return for a name. The minister combed the few books available to him and came upon an account of early exploration on the western lake, translated from French. Thus the Sieur du Lhut was rediscovered and rescued from obscurity by a city named after him.

A national financial panic came in 1857. The settlers in Duluth were ruined, and every store in town closed down. At the age of four, Duluth became a ghost town. What commerce remained in the area moved to Superior, which itself had shrunk to 1,000 residents, a third of its peak size.

Stuntz stayed on, though, and in another nine years his patience was rewarded. He heard reports of a gold strike in the Vermilion area, far to the north. He went to investigate and quickly saw that the deposit was mostly iron pyrites, or "fool's gold." He also noticed that iron ore existed in the vicinity in greater quanitity than he had ever seen before. The area eventually was developed as the Soudan Mine, one of the richest in Minnesota.

Stuntz contacted financier Jay Cooke, who quickly decided to connect the new strike to Duluth by rail. Cooke's announcement had an immediate effect on the town. Businessmen came rushing in to take part in the expected boom, and Duluth was alive again. By 1869, the city had overtaken Superior in population. The next year the Northern Pacific Railroad completed its spur from St. Paul. Its original destination had been Superior, but Cooke's influence brought it to Duluth instead. The decision was a bitter blow to the rival city in Wisconsin, and there was worse to come. The eager newcomers in Duluth had spotted a major flaw in plans for a port development. Minnesota Point was too long. Ships entering the harbor actually were closer to Superior when they cleared the Point. The Duluth contingent was convinced that this geographical fact would give Superior an unbeatable advantage. Fortunately, there was an alternative. A canal near the head of the Point would enable ships to take a shortcut and bring them right into the middle of Duluth. In late 1870, digging of the canal began.

Superior was not about to take this without a fight. The city filed suit and after several months managed to get a federal injunction to stop the work, on the grounds that it would damage the flow of the St. Louis River. Duluth, however, kept right on digging. On April 29, 1871, the steam dredger cutting across the Point stalled on frozen gravel and came to a halt. The city already had learned that federal marshals were on their way to serve the injunction. The entire canal project was in peril. Duluth rose to the occasion. Its citizens poured from their homes with picks and shovels and blasting powder in an all-out effort to finish the canal. On May 2, the dredger and its human assistants reached water on the far side, to the accompaniment of tumultuous cheers. As the injunction to stop the work was served, the steam tug *Frank C. Fero* chugged through the fifteen-foot-wide canal.

Superior didn't give up. The Wisconsin city fought on for three more years, trying every legal stratagem its lawyers could dream up in an effort to thwart Duluth. It was not all that futile a hope. The Minnesota city had been rocked by the panic of 1873, and Cooke's railroad scheme had collapsed. But in 1874, the government ruled that Superior no longer had standing to sue because control of the canal had passed to the federal government. The two cities eventually reconciled and developed the harbor together, but the canal gave Duluth a financial and social ascendancy that it still maintains.

The canal is now a 300-foot-wide ditch, and the aerial lift bridge that crosses it is one of Duluth's best-known landmarks. The bridge, carrying South Lake Street traffic across the canal and onto Minnesota Point, was built in 1905. The platform itself was replaced in 1930, but the overhead structure and towers are part of the original. The 386-foot-long span can be raised 138 feet in just fifty-five seconds to clear the way for ship passages. The lift weighs 900 tons and is counterbalanced by two 450-ton concrete blocks. Canal Park now runs across the Point on the northern side of the canal. At its side is the Lake Superior Marine Museum, with exhibits relating to the lake and Duluth-Superior harbor. A verbal commentary also is given on every ship that comes through the canal. The museum is open daily, mid-May to October, 10:00 to 9:00; the rest of the year, Monday to Saturday, to 4:30. There is no admission charge. Also in the area is an interesting shop specializing in lake antiques, the Bridge and Anchor, at 715 South Lake Avenue.

Beyond the bridge lies Minnesota Point, a unique peninsular community that is part of Duluth, yet quite separate. Amid shifting dunes there are houses which back onto the water. Although the big city is in plain view—just a few miles down the lake—the Point remains far removed from it, in a corner of its own. The road follows this narrow strip of development for about seven miles, ending at Park Point. This public recreational facility has fine views of the busy harbor, the ore and grain docks of Superior, and Duluth's cliffs. Clamber across the dunes to the other side, though, and you face the open lake, without the slightest evidence of a city anywhere in sight. There are picnic grounds, beaches, and playgrounds here. For the rest of its length, Minnesota Point is a natural sanctuary in which the only travel is on foot. Migrating birds flock to the area in season, and there are ample opportunities for solitary hikes in the dunes. At the end of the point are the brick ruins of the old lighthouse that operated here from 1858 to 1878. After the shifting channel was finally fixed, the light was removed. The ruins remain as a reminder that this is the zero point of all marine surveys of Lake Superior.

Split Rock Lighthouse

The North Shore Highway from Duluth to the Canadian border has been one of the great scenic roads in the United States since its opening in 1924. Local tourist literature describes it as "the second most scenic road in America," although it isn't quite clear who was polled on this momentous question or what road came away with the championship. It is a marvelous road all the same, never running too far from the lakeside and at times opening out on splendid views down the bluffs and over the blue water. Waterfalls come tumbling from the hills at intervals, and short walks from the road will bring the traveler to the edge of foaming cascades. The lovely resort town of Grand Marais lies along the route, as does historic Grand Portage National Monument. But of all the places along the road, there is none quite so haunting and powerful as the Split Rock Lighthouse. Perched atop a sheer wall of rock, 138 feet above Superior, the lighthouse occupies a site of glowing beauty.

Long before Split Rock was built, explorers observed that the spot was perfect for a lighthouse. It was in 1854 that surveyor Thomas Clark came by on a surveying trip by canoe and noted the bluff would make an ideal location for a light. But despite repeated pleas for funds by the Minnesota Legislature, it was not until 1892 that the first federal lighthouse was built on the western Lake Superior shore. As was the case with all other projects on the northern lakes, this country was regarded by Congress as being almost comically remote. Although it was acknowledged as a stormy and dangerous coast, water traffic was still comparatively light. Those ships that did pass through the area discovered another uncomfortable fact about the coast: because of the great deposits of iron ore in the hills, ship's compasses did not work correctly. Still, no lighthouse money was forthcoming from Washington.

When a light was finally approved, it was placed at Two Harbors, port for the Vermilion iron mines. It took two forces working in combination to get the Split Rock project approved. The first was the United States Steel Corporation, the most active ship operator in the area. The company began using its considerable influence in Washington for this project in the years after its formation in 1901. Then in 1905 an even stronger force made a statement. A vicious November storm slammed into the lake and wrecked four vessels in the immediate vicinity of Split Rock. That shook the money loose—an appropriation of $75,000—and five years later the lighthouse opened.

Its name does not refer to a cleavage in the rock, but to a natural characteristic of the underlying stone. Bedrock is a dark gray mineral known as diabase. In distant geologic times, a brilliant white stone, anorthosite, was embedded in its midst. The resulting effect appears to be a web of white tendrils splitting apart the black rock.

No road ran along the coast during the years of construction. All material and equipment had to be brought in by boat and then pulled up the face of the sheer 100-foot cliff. A hoisting engine was landed by barge, then lifted up the bluff by block and tackle. It in turn hoisted up a derrick and 310 tons of equipment used in building the lighthouse. A tramway finally replaced the engine in 1916.

The first crude road had been cut through the forests from Duluth in 1915; still it was an isolated existence for the lighthouse keeper. The light closed down in winter, but during the navigation season the keeper seldom saw his family. Three two-story brick homes were built on the site for the keeper and his two assistants, and eventually enough amenities existed to enable families to join the crew. The original beacon, manufactured in Paris, produced a light of 450,000 candlepower. By 1961, it had been replaced by a beacon of 2.5 million candlepower which had a range of twenty-three miles. A foghorn, audible from five miles off, also operated until 1969.

With the opening of the North Shore Highway, Split Rock became known as the most visited lighthouse in the country. The Coast Guard finally had to call a halt in 1951, and closed the tower to visitors because crowds were interfering with work. The lighthouse was deactivated in 1968 and became a Minnesota state park three years later; now the entire complex is fully open again. The Minnesota Historical Society runs the 7.63-acre facility, and guided tours are given through the light tower. The state is restoring the light and its surrounding complex of buildings to their appearance in the years after its 1910 opening. Personnel in period costume are on hand to answer questions.

Be sure to stop at the lookout point, one mile south of the state park entrance. It has the best and most famous view of this majestic beacon, as it stands high above the lake on its solitary bluff. You might even be tempted to give the North Shore Highway, on the strength of that view alone, a higher rating whenever they take the next "most scenic highway" vote.

Other Things to See

[1]   The French discovered the Pigeon River route to the Minnesota interior in 1722, and for nearly a century after that the portage at the river's mouth was one of the focal points of the west. It was called Grand Portage, "the great carrying place." The Montreal-based North West Company used it as its western base and the place for July Rendezvous starting in 1768. After the American Revolution, the place became United States territory, and in 1803 the Montrealers decamped to Fort William, Ontario, to avoid taxation. The stockade has been restored to its late eighteenth-century appearance, and the Great Hall, where the company partners once sat to haggle over shares and strategy, is again its centerpiece. Other buildings on the grounds include a kitchen, canoe warehouse, and cabin, as well as a small museum. The setting is beautiful as well as historic. On clear days Isle Royale National Park is visible on the horizon. (There is daily boat service to that island, mid-June to Labor Day. Check locally for times.) The Grand Portage National Monument is open daily, mid-May to mid-October, 9:00 to 5:00. There is no admission charge.

[2]   Some of the best attractions of the North Shore Highway are the waterfalls that come bubbling down from the hills every few miles. Five state parks have been established along the route of U.S. 61 to preserve some of the more scenic areas. They are: Judge C. R. Magney, on the Arrowhead River, 27 miles south of the Canadian border; Cascade River, a series of rapids in which the river drops 225 feet in one mile, 51 miles south; Temperance River (so named because there is no bar at its mouth), with cascades falling almost to the lakeside, 70 miles south; Baptism River, with the state's highest waterfall and sheer rock cliffs above the lake, 92 miles south; and Gooseberry Falls, with a total drop of 240 feet, 111 miles south.

[3]   Grand Marais is the most picturesque of the North Shore lake towns, with a splendid harbor and fine charter fishing facilities. It also is the access point for some of the best canoeing waters in North America, the Boundary Waters area of Superior National Forest (see Side Trips).

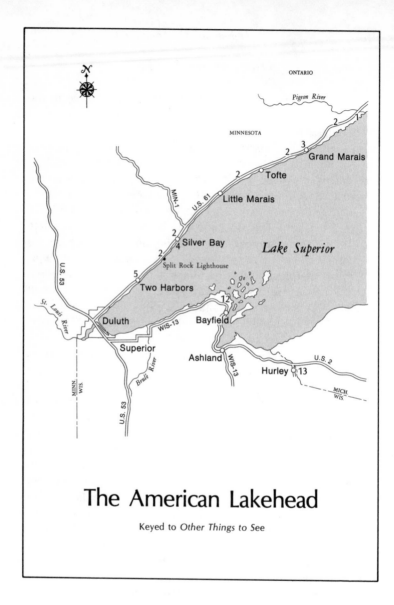

The American Lakehead

Keyed to *Other Things to See*

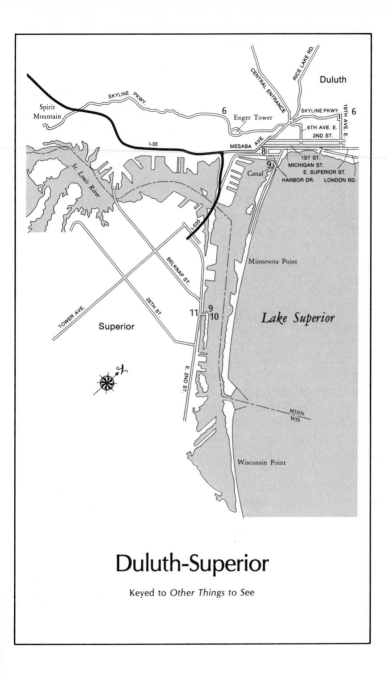

Duluth-Superior

Keyed to *Other Things to See*

[4]   This part of the lakeshore is taconite country. The low-grade iron ore is brought to refineries here from mines in the interior. The taconite industry has brought a degree of prosperity to this part of the state; but, at Silver Bay, it also has resulted in the worst pollution on Lake Superior. The plant there, built in 1956, produces 10.5 million tons of taconite pellets each year. You can watch them being loaded on freighters at Taconite Harbor, operated by the Erie Mining Company.

[5]   Plans for a railroad between the Vermilion iron mines and Duluth were smashed when financier Jay Cooke went bankrupt during the panic of 1873. However, Charlemagne Tower of Pottsville, Pennsylvania, took over Cooke's scheme and completed the railroad in 1884. Instead of Duluth, he made Two Harbors the terminus of the Duluth and Iron Range Railroad, a switch that slowed down Duluth's growth hardly at all and made tiny Two Harbors a rich little town. The depot of that railroad, built in 1907, is now the Lake County Historical and Railroad Museum, with exhibits relating to the town's history and the construction of the seventy-mile-long rail line. There are also views of the ore docks from adjacent Van Hoven Park. The museum is open May to October, Monday through Saturday, 9:00 to 4:00; Sunday, 1:00 to 4:00. A donation is asked.

[6]   Skyline Parkway follows the rim of the bluffs above Duluth for thirty miles, affording a continuous scenic drive overlooking the city and the harbor. There are several turnouts and recreational areas en route. Near the drive's western end is Spirit Mountain, a vast complex developed by the city of Duluth. The park is open year round, with a complete assortment of summer activities from tennis to horseback riding. In winter, Spirit Mountain becomes a skiing complex with fourteen downhill runs, cross country courses, and five chairlifts. The runs usually operate from Thanksgiving to March. The chairlifts also run from mid-June to mid-September, so summertime visitors can take a look. The best free viewpoint on the Skyline Drive is the Enger Tower, at Eighteenth Avenue West. The sixty-foot-high lookout atop Enger Peak was dedicated in 1939 by Crown Prince Olav of Norway (later to become King Olav V).

[7]   Duluth's Norwegian roots are also celebrated at Leif

Erickson Park, on U.S. 61 at Eleventh Avenue East. Besides its fine rose gardens, the park contains a replica of the ship in which the Viking explorer sailed to North America in the tenth century. The modern craft was actually sailed across the Atlantic from Bergen, Norway, to New York, and was presented to Duluth by Capt. Gerhard Folgero in 1927.

[8]   Many cities have been faced with the problem of what to do with an aging railroad depot when the trains stop running. Duluth's solution may be the best. It turned the old Union Depot, built in 1890, into the St. Louis County Heritage and Arts Center, housing three museums and headquarters for many of the city's cultural groups. Within the former depot are the A. M. Chisholm Museum of Oriental art and natural history; the St. Louis County Historical Society, with exhibits on the rich pioneer life of northern Minnesota; and the Lake Superior Museum of Transportation and Industry, a collection of rail memorabilia. There are also studios, workshops, and theaters throughout the building. Located just west of the road to Minnesota Point, at 506 West Michigan, the building is open 10:00 to 5:00, Monday through Saturday; 1:00 to 5:00 on Sunday. There is an admission charge.

[9]   Boat tours of Duluth-Superior's impressive harbor leave from both sides of the state line. The trips cover essentially the same territory, with the high point being the Farmers Union grain elevator, towering 285 feet above the water at the foot of Tower Avenue in Superior. The cruises leave from Duluth at the foot of Fifth Avenue West, daily, June to mid-October, 9:30 to 9:30. In Superior, cruises depart from Barker's Island, accessible by bridge from Sixth Avenue East off U.S. 2 and 53. These trips run from June to mid-September, 10:30 to 6:30. Fares are approximately the same for both cruises, and each lasts about two hours.

[**10**]   Also on Superior's Barker's Island is the S.S. *Meteor,* the last of the forty-three whaleback freighters that once sailed on the Great Lakes. This vessel with its distinctive rounded hull was built in Superior in 1896 and served until 1971. It is now a museum of Great Lakes commerce. Tours are offered daily, Memorial Day to Labor Day. Before mid-June, they operate from 10:00 to 5:00; afterward from 9:00 to 7:00. There is an admission charge. The island itself is a sixty-five-acre facility built from sand

dredged up from the harbor channel in the early years of this century. A group of small shops operate near the *Meteor,* and plans call for construction of a marina and hotel on the site, too.

[11]   The home of lumber baron Martin Pattison has been turned into a museum of Superior's pioneer days and of Lake Superior history. The Douglas County Historical Museum, at 906 East Second Street, also contains exhibits of antique musical instruments and Japanese ceramics. It is open May to September, 9:00 to 5:00; weekends, 1:30 to 5:00. In March and April, it is closed Monday and operates from 9:00 to noon and 1:00 to 4:30 on weekdays, 1:30 to 4:30 on Saturday, and 2:00 to 4:30 on Sunday.

[12]   The Red Cliff Indian Reservation preserves the remnant of Chippewa culture that remains on the shores of Chequamegon Bay. The Cultural Center in Red Cliff on Wisconsin 13, three miles north of Bayfield, displays handicrafts and historical exhibits relating to the tribe. Many similar items are offered for sale in the museum shop. Exhibits are grouped around a spiral ramp in the handsome museum building. Check locally for hours. There is an admission charge.

[13]   Among the half dozen or so towns that once bore the title "wickedest city in the North," Hurley probably had as much claim as any to the crown. During the 1890s and into the Prohibition era, Hurley's Silver Street was famous for its dens of liquor, vice, and iniquity. An impressive collection of saloons remains along the length of this once notorious street, but the vice has mostly disappeared. Although a few of the clubs there even offer children's menus, one may still quench a thirst with no trouble whatsoever.

Side Trips

Canoeists claim that the Boundary Waters of the Superior National Forest, northwest of Grand Marais, provide the best canoeing area in the country. No motorized boats are permitted in this wilderness, and for those who want to feel what this country was like when the voyageurs traveled the dark, silent waters, a trip into this area is a close approximation. Outfitters and guides are available in Grand Marais. For those who only

The whaleback freighter S.S. *Meteor*, on Superior's Barker's Island, sailed the Great Lakes for seventy-five years. *Courtesy Wisconsin Division of Tourism.*

want to explore by car, the Gunflint Trail is a fifty-eight-mile scenic road that winds past lakes and streams on the way from Grand Marais to Saganaga Lake and access to the Boundary Waters. The area adjoins Quetico Provincial Park in Ontario. For information on travel permits and border crossing regulations, write the Forest Supervisor of Superior National Forest, Box 338, Duluth 55801.

Virginia, sixty-five miles north of Duluth on U.S. 53, lies near the center of the great Minnesota iron ranges. Views of open pit mining are available south of town at the Rouchleau Mine, open June to Labor Day, 9:00 to 8:00. There is an admission charge. In Chisholm, eighteen miles west on U.S. 169, is the Iron Range Interpretive Center, with displays illustrating the history and social and economic impact of the great Mesabi strikes. It is open daily, 10:00 to 6:00; mid-May to mid-October, 9:00 to 9:00. There is an admission charge. In Soudan, twenty-eight miles northeast of Virginia on Minnesota 169, is Tower Soudan State Park, preserving the state's first iron mine which operated from 1882 to 1962. Tours are given through the underground passages, open pits, and various buildings on the site. The park is open from mid-May to September, 9:00 to 4:00; in early May, 11:00 to 4:00. There is an admission charge.

Chequamegon National Forest covers 839,000 acres south of Ashland along U.S. 63 and Wisconsin 13. Like the Superior National Forest in Minnesota, this is fine canoeing country with many streams and lakes flowing into each other along the Flambeau and Chippewa rivers. The best scenic drive runs west from Clam Lake on Bayfield County Road M to Cable, forty-three miles southwest of Ashland. The road goes by the Telemark Ski Area, which has three chair lifts and operates from late November to mid-April. The region also is storied among fishermen for its muskies, with the record-holding sixty-nine-pounder having been taken from these waters.

State Parks on the Lake

The parks lying along the North Shore Highway between Duluth and the Canadian border are described in Other Things to See. Four of the five parks have camping facilities, the exception being Baptism River. At Judge C. R. Magney, 18 miles northeast of Grand Marais, there are 39 tent spaces. In Cascade River, 10 miles southwest of Grand Marais, there are 45 campsites; and in Temperance River, 23 miles southwest of Grand Marais, there are 50 campsites. In Gooseberry Falls, 13 miles northeast of Two Harbors, there are 125 tent spaces. All the parks also have fishing.

Big Bay, at the southeastern tip of Madeline Island, is a 1,288-acre facility, with a 1.5 mile sand beach, hiking trails, rock formations, and a marsh (in an undeveloped section of the island). There are 18 campsites.

Copper Harbor is situated at the tip of Michigan's Keweenaw Peninsula. *Courtesy the* Detroit News.

4

Vein of Copper

In the spring of 1840, a young Detroit physician, Douglass Houghton, arrived in the western part of Michigan's Upper Peninsula on a self-promoted mission as state geologist. Michigan had received this enormous tract of wilderness as compensation for surrendering Toledo to the state of Ohio. Actually, the proposition as framed by President Andrew Jackson had been "take it or else." The president had made it quite clear that unless Michigan acceded, there would be no statehood in the foreseeable future. Although Wisconsin was under the impression that the peninsula belonged to her, Michigan grudgingly accepted it and entered the Union in 1837. The dominant view in the state was that the Upper Peninsula was totally worthless and should be ignored.

Houghton did not agree. His training had been in botany, and he had come to Detroit to give lectures in natural science. He became so popular in the frontier town, though, that he settled in to practice medicine and dentistry. In 1830 he had accompanied the Henry Schoolcraft expedition into the region that would soon become part of Michigan. Although he was not a geologist, he was convinced that he had seen enormous quantities of copper lying near the surface in the areas near Lake Superior.

Houghton had not been the first man to see such things. Copper had been something of a northern El Dorado since the earliest days of European exploration. When Samuel de Champlain first made contact with the western Indians, they told him stories of islands made of solid copper and giant copper boulders lying on the southern shore of a great lake. Champlain, although he would have preferred to find gold and silver, was nonetheless intrigued. Subsequent expeditions into the western lakes were instructed to be on the lookout for these copper deposits. They did turn up some evidence. Ancient mine pits could be seen at several places along the lake, and reports of copper artifacts would turn up from as far away as the prehistoric Hopewell Mounds of Ohio; but the current inhabitants of the region knew nothing of these vanished miners. By the late seventeenth century the French were sure there was copper on Isle Royale, and one explorer claimed to have seen a boulder of copper on the Ontonagon River. In 1727, Louis Denis, Sieur de la Ronde, attempted to exploit deposits he had found on Madeline Island, Wisconsin. Mining experts were sent out from France to verify the presence of copper, but the vein petered out without producing much wealth.

When the British took over the country, they heard many of the same legends. Jonathan Carver repeated them in embellished form in a book on the area published in 1770. It caused a sensation in London. A group of wealthy noblemen formed a corporation to find these riches and sent out a party under Mackinac trader Alexander Henry. They sunk a few shafts along the Ontonagon, failed to find much of anything, and gave up. Still the tales persisted. Veteran copper men even say that at the Treaty of Paris, at which the United States-British border was drawn after the Revolutionary War, Benjamin Franklin insisted that Isle Royale be placed on the American side of the border because he believed it was the island of copper of the old legends. Although the island is much closer to the Canadian mainland, the British wearily acceded, saying that if the talks went on much longer, Franklin probably would start demanding Ireland, too.

By 1840, most of that had been forgotten or discounted. When young Houghton asked his friend, Gov. Stephens T. Mason, to allow him to explore the area for mineral development, the governor agreed more in the spirit of friendship than commerce. Houghton was granted $3,000 and told to have a nice time. All through the year he explored the hooked finger of the Keweenaw Peninsula, and by December of 1840 he had prepared his report. It was purposely understated. The land had not yet been properly surveyed and still belonged to the Chippewa. Houghton did not want to touch off a copper rush. The California gold frenzy was still nine years in the future, but Houghton feared the excesses that fortune-hunters would inflict on the land if the word went out prematurely. Nevertheless, the bare facts were enough. He wrote: "With a single blast I threw out nearly two tons of ore. With this there were many masses of native copper from the most minute specks to one of about forty pounds in weight." Congress immediately concluded a treaty with the Chippewa, gaining 25,000 square miles of land along the lakeshore in Michigan, Wisconsin, and Minnesota. Washington also decided to supplement Houghton's grant so that he could make a complete survey of the area, preparing the way for the staking out of claims.

Congress acted none too soon. The first miners made their way to the Keweenaw by boat from the Soo in 1841. By 1843 the trickle had turned into a rush. Greater numbers of men came to seek Michigan copper than went to seek California gold, but the results were not as dramatic. It would take a good deal of capital and technology to mine the underground veins of the Keweenaw, although that was not fully understood at first. After the initial surface copper was picked off, there wasn't much more an individual could do. The overwhelming majority went home with nothing. As the mines developed, however, immigrants streamed to the area from Finland and the Cornwall region of England (in which copper had been mined for generations). These arrivals gave the Copper Country an ethnic identity that survives to this day. The pasty, the meat pie that Cornish miners took with them underground for lunch, is still a staple on area menus and the most famous local dish. And you only have to read the signs on the storefronts to recognize the continuing Finnish presence here. The sauna is a long-standing tradition in this part of Michigan. More notably, Suomi College in Hancock was founded in 1896 to educate the children of the Finnish immigrants.

The first big copper strike was made in 1844 near what is now the town of Phoenix. Discovery of the Cliff Mine ended the days of random searching and brought in big money and institutionalized mining. There were fortunes to be made for those with the capital to invest. According to one history of the copper country, a 500-share piece of the Cliff, purchased for $9,000 in 1845, would have returned $255,000 by 1858. The Cliff was not even part of the main lode—it was on overflow that had been forced to the surface at right angles to the main body of copper—but it was almost pure copper, unlike anything ever seen before on the continent. No smelting was required. To veteran miners it bordered on the miraculous. The Cliff was played out by 1880, after giving up 40 million pounds of copper. The big strike would not be made until 1864 when Edwin J. Hulbert hit the Calumet lode; but the Cliff Mine established copper mining as a profitable industry and attracted eastern money, coming primarily from Boston, that developed the Michigan mines.

By the start of the Civil War, Michigan was producing 15 million pounds of copper a year, or 89.5 percent of the national total. It was one of the decisive industrial factors in the Union's war effort. Between 1850 and 1884, the mines turned out nearly three-quarters of all copper mined in America, and in the 1880s they produced 15 percent of the total in the entire world. After that, though, new strikes in Montana and Arizona reduced the state's share of the market. Although production reached a peak of 266 million pounds in 1916, that was only 13 percent of the national total. By the end of World War II, production was down to 43 million pounds and the percentage had sunk to 3.6 of total United States production. Since a prolonged strike finally closed the Calumet and Hecla Mines in 1968, copper production has been negligible. Yet the memories remain bright.

Houghton, the man who touched off this rush for riches, never enjoyed any of them. A year after the Cliff Mine was discovered, while on an October surveying trip down the western side of the Keweenaw, he was drowned off Eagle River in a sudden storm. His body was not recovered until the following spring. There is a small monument to him in Eagle River. Fittingly, the town of Houghton keeps his name alive—the town and the deserted shafts of dozens of mines that run the entire length of the Keweenaw, in a land once thought worthless.

The rugged Keweenaw Peninsula shoreline confronts the vastness of Lake Superior. *Photo by Ellen Barnes, courtesy of* Michigan Living/AAA Motor News.

Copper Harbor

Copper Harbor has always been a very long way from anywhere. Although it shares the same state with Detroit, for instance, the distance between the two places is 595 miles—or slightly greater than the distance between Detroit and Washington, D.C. The town sits at the very tip of the Keweenaw Peninsula with nothing around it but Lake Superior. In summer it can be a very lively little place. Several resorts are located in the vicinity, and it is the main point of departure for boat trips to Isle Royale National Park. But when the Lake Superior winter closes in, even hardy Upper Peninsula natives retreat to more congenial places. Many who live here in summer to serve the tourist trade maintain a second home in Hancock or Houghton for the months between October and May. Then Copper Harbor dwindles to about twenty people, the one-room schoolhouse becomes the center of activity, and the click of the traffic flasher (the only stoplight in all of Keweenaw County) can be heard all through the icy, empty town.

Keweenaw is Michigan's smallest county, in both area and population. A sign on the cash register of a Copper Harbor restaurant advises that no personal checks are accepted because the nearest bank is twenty-eight miles away in Mohawk. There isn't even a practicing attorney in the county. The prosecutor, who works as an attorney in Hancock, in neighboring Houghton County, fills the job part-time in Keweenaw. Not much ever happens in the Keweenaw, so there really isn't a great deal for him to do there. The most violent action around is the waves slapping in on long, rock-strewn beaches. The liveliest event in recent memory was a fire in a deserted summer cabin which reached a store of ammunition and kept the firemen pinned down for a good half hour. But Copper Harbor wasn't always peaceful; in the 1840s it was as wild a mining town as any of the legendary western hellholes. Within a few years, mining activities moved far down the peninsula, and Copper Harbor assumed its present serene guise. But it had its moments.

Even in the 1840s it was a long way from anywhere, probably even a longer way than now. It is a tribute to the drawing power of copper that so many men would flock to this remote location to try their luck. It was actually an advertisement of sorts that drew them—a two-ton boulder of solid copper taken out of the Upper Peninsula for all to see. The boulder had been described by Indians to the first French explorers, and a few voyageurs told dubious Quebec officials of seeing this wonder themselves. Later expeditions verified its existence on the Ontonagon River, west of the Keweenaw. In 1843, as news of the copper finds in the north began to excite the rest of Michigan, Detroit businessman Julius Eldred was struck with the bright idea of moving this boulder to the big cities and charging admission to see it. He went north, located the rock, and bought it from the local Chippewas for $150. The only problem was that woodsman Jim Paul was also under the impression that he had obtained rights to the boulder. In the midst of their arguments, Secretary of War James M. Porter declared that the fabulous boulder belonged to the American people and demanded that it be handed over for transport to Washington. Paul told the Army major delegated to seize the boulder to take a quick jump in Lake Superior. But Eldred, a very determined man, made a second payment to Paul to obtain the copper. He loaded it on a ship and set sail for Detroit. Waiting for him there was a Navy cutter with orders to transport the boulder to Washington. A dejected Eldred sailed with his twice-bought prize all the way to the Capital before giving up and going home. (Today the boulder is the property of the Smithsonian Institution.) These events and the exhibition of the giant copper rock caused a sensation in the east and helped fuel the great rush to the Upper Peninsula.

The War Department, having intervened in the weighty matter of the boulder, made a more substantial contribution in 1844. Upon the urging of Michigan's congressional delegation, the new Secretary of War, William Wilkins, sent 105 men of the United States Fifth Infantry to garrison a fort at Copper Harbor, safeguard federal claims in the area, and protect miners from possibly hostile Indians. The Indians proved more indifferent than unfriendly, and the most unsettling event of Fort Wilkins's first year was the wrecking of its supply ship in the harbor. That eventually led to the construction of a lighthouse at the harbor entrance in 1849, but by that time the troops already had left. (At the outbreak of the Mexican War in 1846, the Fort Wilkins garrison was withdrawn and sent into action.) Twenty-one years later, during a temporary overflow of men in Great Lakes area army posts, the fort was manned for a second time. This garrison remained until 1870, when the troops left permanently. For its entire history, Fort Wilkins was occupied a total of five years. It was never engaged in anything resembling warlike activity. Its only enemy was the boredom of the interminable winter. The deserted fort entered the new century as a local curiosity and popular picnic place until the state of Michigan acquired the site in 1923 as a historic park. It has been restored to its appearance of the 1840s, and guides in period uniforms now recreate the ambience of a frontier outpost of that era.

The fort is situated on a narrow neck of land that faces the inland Lake Fanny Hooe. The lake was given its name by the first garrison, which sought to honor the Virginia-born sister-in-law of 1st Lt. Daniel Ruggles. Miss Hooe had accompanied her pregnant sister to the remote outpost to assist with her delivery. Ruggles used his time there to make scientific studies of the Keweenaw and its lake tides. He served with honor in the Mexican War and eventually became a major general in the Confederate Army. Miss Hooe returned to Virginia and raised a family of her own. The fort is located one mile east of Copper Harbor on U.S. 41. It is open daily, mid-May to mid-October. There is an admission charge.

Also a part of the state park is the Copper Harbor Lighthouse, built in 1866 to replace the first structure on the site. It was in turn replaced by an automated light tower in 1933 and is now a museum. The light is accessible by foot trail from Fort Wilkins, but it is not an especially easy walk. More convenient are the cruises that leave hourly from the state marina on the west end of town. They run from July to Labor Day, daily, 10:00 to 5:00. There is a charge. The light contains exhibits on nineteenth-century Great Lakes shipping and the life of a lighthouse keeper of that period.

There are two other short, interesting trips to take from Copper Harbor. Brockway Mountain Drive begins just west of town

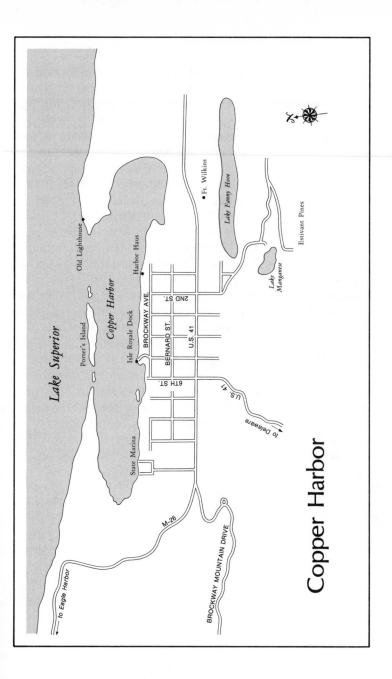

Copper Harbor

and leads to an overlook 735 feet above the lake. It is a spectacular viewpoint over miles of pine forest and water, especially striking at twilight with the sun descending upon the water. The mountain was named for a pioneer hotel owner, D. D. Brockway. He purchased the government land claims office that was situated on Porter Island across the harbor, and transported it to the mainland. A portion of that structure survives as the Harbor Haus Restaurant, a pleasant establishment at the foot of First Street serving German food.

Another scenic trip leads to Estivant Pines, one of the last stands of virgin white pine that remains in Michigan. White pine is the majestic tree that supported the state's lumber industry. Most forests like Estivant Pines were wiped out during the excesses of the nineteenth century. This one was in the process of being eradicated as late as 1971, until the Michigan Nature Association mounted a successful campaign to save it. The MNA bought the 200-acre preserve for $42,000 as a sanctuary. The largest tree in the area measures 23 feet around and 120 feet in height. The Pines are accessible only by foot trail from the end of Manganese Lake Road, east of town, off U.S. 41. It is advisable to obtain a map and good directions in Copper Harbor. The Pines are intended to be a true wilderness experience, and all motorized vehicles and overnight camping are prohibited.

Copper Ghosts

The boom is over in Michigan's Copper Country; all that remains is a long silence. Calumet and Hecla Mines, the economic pillar of the area, closed up in 1968. The Calumet district, which once supported a population of 66,000, now has barely one-tenth that number. Ruins of mines abandoned long ago dot the countryside. Although the party has clearly ended, no one wants to say a last good-bye. Those that have chosen to remain in the Copper Country stubbornly hang on and hope for better days. Plans are being made for a major tourist complex—called Coppertown USA—to be built around the Calumet and Hecla offices. A sizable group of retirees, forced to leave years ago to find work in the auto plants of the Lower Peninsula, are slowly returning to live out their years in the towns of their youth. The twin cities of Hancock and Houghton have become a small but lively cultural center. Several professional people, the grandchildren of immigrant miners, went away to school but came home to practice. In some cases they made a sizable sacrifice in income to do it. None of them seems to regret it.

Copper Country is a beautiful land, touched with a wistful sadness that only seems to heighten its appeal for those who know it. It is filled with haunting echoes and wispy shadows. A fast sampling of some Copper Country ghosts will give you some understanding of the hold it has on its people. The trip leads from a Keweenaw ghost town to a former mine in nearby Ontonagon County. En route, it stops in Calumet and at a remarkable piece of mining machinery near Hancock. The trip can be done in one day, but two would be better. You set your own pace. It is that kind of country.

Start at Central Mine, about halfway between Calumet and Copper Harbor on U.S. 41, the road that runs up the spine of the Keweenaw. This was one of the first big mines to open here, dating from 1854. Like the nearby Cliff Mine, it was a "mass" mine, turing up copper in metallic chunks rather than conglomerate. Not only was its copper pure, it was also plentiful. In its first year of operation the Central returned a dividend to its shareholders, a remarkable record considering the high start-up costs of a mine.

The opening of the Central coincided with the great influx of Cornish miners to Copper Country. They flocked to the place and gave the town of 1,200 the look and sound of a piece of Cornwall. In 1869 they built a Methodist church and filled it each Sunday with song and sermon. For thirty years it was a lively little place. But the Central, like most of the early mines, was built over a fissure off the main copper lode. By 1898 it was played out, and within three years Central Mine was deserted. The homes and stores that once stood there crumbled to ruin and the grass grew over their foundations.

The church remained, however, and in 1907 a strange tradition began. On the last Sunday of July, the Cornish former residents of the town returned to the empty streets and held memorial services in the church. They gathered here annually from all over the country. As years went on, those who actually had lived in Central Mine passed on, but their children and grandchildren continued to keep the appointment in July. Gradually the picnics and other activities that accompanied the first reunions were replaced by a simple church service. Reunion day is now the only day of the year on which the church is opened. A collection is made then for the care of the building and adjacent burial ground for the coming year. If you are not there on reunion day, you can peer in through the windows at the interior, then poke around the graveyard and scattered stones of what was once a town. It is the most intriguing of the Copper Country ghosts.

Continue south to Calumet, once the greatest city of the Michigan North and now a town of barely 1,000 residents. In the boom days this area was a patchwork of little communities, and the business district of what is now Calumet was called Red Jacket. It offered the sort of amenities not to be found within hundreds of miles. The Calumet and Hecla ran everything in the area with the benevolent paternalism of the wealthy Bostonians who owned the company. Medical care was excellent, and kindergarten classes began here long before most American cities had them. The company established a fine 16,000-volume library, built an elegant 1,100-seat opera house in 1900 that hosted the greatest names in the theater, and paved a section of the downtown streets in 1906—the first concrete pavement in the state. Its wage rates were generally higher than those prevailing throughout the east. Only steady dividends from the mines and Republican majorities at election time were expected in return.

The dividends were never in doubt. By the end of World War II, when it had become the last copper producer in the area, Calumet and Hecla had paid out more than $200 million in dividends. That represented 57 percent of all dividends paid out by all mines in the Copper Country. It had also produced 48 percent of all the copper mined in the area. Edwin Hulbert, member of a well-to-do Detroit family, had discovered the lode and brought in the wealthy Bostonians who could raise the capital to operate it. Hulbert, however, lost his interest in the mine in unwise investments in other Copper Country enterprises. (Even then his Boston friends made sure he received a healthy settlement to live on. They were not a mean-spirited crowd.) He was replaced as manager of the mine by Alexander Agassiz, son of the famous naturalist Louis Agassiz and a brother-in-law of the chief investor. It was under his management that the mine reached its greatest prosperity.

You can walk along Fifth and Sixth streets today, the main arteries of the business district, and get an idea of what a dazzling place this used to be. Many of the fine old stores have become galleries specializing in copper artworks. The opera house has been restored and presents a variety of summer attractions. The wonderful Victorian excesses of the business facades are quite photogenic. It is a fine place for discovery and aimless strolling, one of the most atmospheric cities in the North. A walk in almost any direction will take you to mementoes of the city's expansive past. Although not exactly a ghost, Calumet's shadows are long.

The former Calumet and Hecla offices are slowly being developed into Coppertown USA, a museum of the boom era and an ethnic theme center, by a nonprofit corporation. Eventually, there will be copper industry exhibition centers, a shopping plaza in the former roundhouse, a reconstructed miners' village, a hotel, and a cultural center. The former library is now the project's administrative offices and contains historical displays and outlines of the proposed complex. It is located off U.S. 41 on the eastern edge of town.

In the early years of copper mining, horsepower alone was enough to raise the ore from shallow pits to the surface. As the "mass" mines were exhausted, it became necessary to dig ever deeper for the ore. The end result can be seen at the site of the old Quincy Mine, on the hill above Hancock on U.S. 41. The mine opened in 1848 and during its peak years was known as "Old Reliable" because it never missed paying a dividend from 1867 to 1921. By the end of that string the copper was becoming less accessible, so in 1920 the company opened its new steam hoist at Number Two Shaft.

This gigantic steam engine, designed by Bruno Nordberg, became the marvel of the mining industry. It cost $371,000 to build. It was sixty feet high, weighed 1.76 million pounds, and could raise ten tons of ore at the speed of 3,200 feet per minute, or about forty miles an hour. At peak operating capacity, it could reach 6,310 feet below the earth's surface. The machine was the wonder of its time and remains an overwhelming sight. Its very existence, however, indicated trouble ahead for the Old Reliable. If mines had to go that deep, the ore was undeniably running out. By 1931 the hoist was out of operation; thirteen years later the Quincy shut down for good. The hoist is open for tours from mid-June to Labor Day, daily, 9:00 to 5:00. There is an admission charge. There is also some antique rail stock from the mines there, and the grounds provide views over the Hancock-Houghton area.

Last on the trip is a tour through a mine itself. There are three onetime mines offering tours. Two of them are the Delaware in Keweenaw County and the Arcadian near Hancock. The best choice, however, is the third, the Adventure. It is near the town of Greenland, thirty-five miles southwest of Houghton on Michigan Highways 26 and 38. The mine was not a money-maker. In fact, to the despair of its owners, it never paid a dividend over ninety years of sporadic operation. It may have done better for the prehistoric miners who also worked it—but they left no financial records.

Visitors ride to the hillside entrance of the Adventure on a tractor-train and then don hardhats for the descent into the interior, miner's lanterns held firmly in hand. It is an informative and realistic tour, a slight taste of the life copper miners led. The mines here were far safer than coal operations in the east, but it was still a dark and cold existence. This tour will show you what it was like, and mine owner and head guide Jack Neph is himself a mine of information on the industry. The Adventure Mine is open from late May to mid-October, daily, 9:00 to 5:00. There is an admission charge.

The Arcadian Mine is one of three copper mines where tourists can catch a glimpse of the Upper Peninsula's once-booming industry. *Courtesy the* Detroit News.

Isle Royale National Park

During the long campaign to make Isle Royale a part of the national park system, Michigan's United States Sen. Arthur Vandenberg expressed shining hopes for the island's coming popularity. "Isle Royale is destined to be one of the greatest, if not the greatest, of all our national parks," he said in 1931, nine years before it became a park. "I expect . . . it to become Michigan's greatest outdoor asset and one of America's most popular objectives." The senator was wrong. Isle Royale remains one of the least visited national parks in the forty-eight contiguous states. Access to the park is severely restricted, and overnight accommodations in something other than a campground are limited to one hundred roooms in two lodges. It is hard to argue with this isolationist policy. Any easing of access or growth of overnight conveniences and tourist pressures would surely destroy the very qualities that make Isle Royale a special place.

It is not a park that can be enjoyed easily by looking from a car window or walking through a museum. It demands active participation in the wilderness experience to understand what the park is all about. It is a place for campers, backpackers, and boaters who come to find the sort of isolated existence that has virtually disappeared from the Great Lakes. The Park Service is serious about preserving this atmosphere. Even such pastimes as frisbee playing and group singing are discouraged as detracting from the place's spirt.

The island is fifty-six miles from the Michigan mainland (the state to which it is nominally attached), twenty-two miles from Minnesota and forty-four miles from Ontario. There are daily boat trips from Copper Harbor and Houghton, Michigan, and Grand Portage, Minnesota, as well as seaplane service from Houghton. It is possible to come over for the day and return to the mainland without remaining overnight. You will get a very nice lake cruise, and if you sail from Copper Harbor to Rock Harbor, the rangers have scheduled a short nature walk through the area which can be completed in time for the boat's departure. But you will get only the slightest taste of the island that way. It is better to stay the night in the lodge at Rock Harbor on the eastern

A moose roams in the unspoiled wilderness preserved by Isle Royale National Park. *Photo by Tom Buchkoe.*

shore or at Windigo on the west, to feel the stillness and look out at a night that scatters stars to the horizons. It is best of all to stay a week, pitch a tent by a lake deep in the interior, and simply put aside for seven days the irritations of an unsettling century.

The French came upon Isle Royale in 1671 and gave it the distinguished name that no one since has seen fit to change. The first explorations uncovered ample evidence of copper workings. Modern archaeology has traced them back 4,500 years, but all the French knew was that the oldest Indian in the area couldn't tell them who had dug these pits. The idea of copper riches here haunted the island's owners for the next two centuries. There were tales that its foundation was solid copper, and Benjamin Franklin insisted on its inclusion on the American side of the post-Revolution boundary line. In 1843, when the copper rush began on the Michigan mainland, prospectors swarmed across Isle Royale. Some mining continued on the island until 1899. Despite all the old legends, no great lode was ever discovered, and eventually the miners gave up. After 1900 it became a summer place, and several cottages were built along the shore. It could have gone the way of a Mackinac or Put-in-Bay and become a resort. But these were the years of the conservation movement's birth, and in the minds of many people its greatest value was as a wilderness retreat rather than a holiday resort.

For the next twenty years, the future of Isle Royale hung in the balance. More cottages were built, but the Island Copper Company still retained title to sizable holdings in the interior, hindering any great development. It was then that Detroit newspaperman Bert Stoll visited the island and was deeply moved by its serenity and distance from the tumult of the mainland. In 1921, he enlisted his paper, the *Detroit News,* in a campaign to preserve the place as a national park. Two years later, Island Copper agreed to donate its land as part of a wilderness park, and in 1924 all private land transactions on the island were stopped. The director of the National Park Service, Stephen T. Mather, paid a visit that year and came away impressed. "I shall take away a deep and lasting impression of this country of the French voyageurs, of the primeval forest. It would make the finest water and trail park I can think of," he said.

The process of acquiring land and ceding it to the federal government took sixteen years. Finally, in 1940 Isle Royale National Park was opened to preserve the beauties that had so enthralled Stoll and Mather. The island today permits no wheeled vehicles—and provides no roads for them to run upon. There are, however, 163 miles of foot trails leading to 31 campgrounds with 192 tent spaces. One of them, on Birch Island, off the northern shore of Isle Royale, has only one tent space for those who are intent on playing Robinson Crusoe. The Park Service does not recommend making the Lake Superior crossing in any boat smaller than twenty feet in length. But such craft can be carried aboard the Park Service boat from Houghton, and canoes are transported on the other boats.

The animal life on the forty-five-mile-long island is limited to those that could fly or swim from the mainland or walk across the winter ice bridge. A herd of moose used the ice bridge around 1900, and is one of the great photographic prizes of the island. A wolf pack also made it to Isle Royale and preys upon the moose. The wolves are only rarely glimpsed by humans. There are both hardwood and evergreen stands on the island. There are also mosquitoes and black flies which, fortunately, diminish after July 1. The season runs from Mid-May to mid-October. Lodge accommodations are available from the third weekend in June to Labor Day.

Three boat services make the trip to Isle Royale during the summer. The largest is the National Park Service's *Ranger III,* a 125-passenger boat running between Houghton and Rock Harbor. Trips to the island are made on Tuesday, Thursday, and Saturday with return trips Wednesday, Friday, and Sunday. There are no Monday trips. Departure time is 9:30 A.M., and the crossing takes six hours. Advance reservations may be made with the Superintendent, Isle Royale National Park, Houghton, Michigan 49931.

The *Isle Royale Queen,* carrying sixty passengers, leaves every day but Sunday from Copper Harbor at 8:00 A.M. for the four-hour trip to Rock Harbor. Return trips sail at 3:30 P.M. Reservations address is Isle Royale Ferry, Copper Harbor, Michigan 49918.

Two boats make the run from Grand Portage. The forty-eight-foot *Voyageur* visits Windigo Inn, then makes an overnight stay at Rock Harbor Lodge before returning to the mainland. It leaves Grand Portage at 9:30 A.M. on Monday, Wednesday, and Saturday, and departs the island at 8:00 A.M. on Tuesday, Thursday, and Sunday for Windigo and the mainland. There are no Friday voyages. Its sister vessel, the 150-passenger *Wenonah,* runs daily between Grand Portage and Windigo. It leaves the mainland at 9:30 A.M. and returns home at 3:00 P.M. Reservations for both vessels may be made with Sivertson Brothers, 366 Lake Avenue, South Duluth, Minnesota 55802.

Float plane service connects both Rock Harbor and Windigo with Houghton. For schedule, rate, and reservations contact the Isle Royale Seaplane Service, P.O. Box 371, Houghton, Michigan 49931.

Other Things to See

[1]   The last iron mine in Ironwood closed in 1967, but for nearly a century before that it was the center of the Gogebic Iron Range. Now the city has become the center of one of the great skiing areas in the Midwest. Mt. Zion, just outside of town on U.S. 2, is one of the tallest peaks in the Gogebic range, at 1,750 feet. It operates for skiing December through April; in the summer a road to the summit leads to a viewpoint over the area and nearby Lake Superior. A larger skiing complex operates at Big Powderhorn, four miles east of town on U.S. 2. It has five double chair lifts and runs from Thanksgiving to early April.

[2]   Little Girl's Point is a very pleasant picnic area on Lake Superior, eighteen miles north of Ironwood on Gogebic County Road 505. There is an agate beach there and a fine viewpoint down the lake from atop the bluffs.

[3]   Ottawa National Forest takes in almost 950,000 acres south and east of Ironwood. A small portion of it also extends along the lakeshore, and the road through the forest to Black River Harbor is a splendid scenic drive. Turnoffs lead to four waterfalls along the way, all of them fairly close to the highway, and short scenic paths lead to various viewpoints along the river. The harbor itself is a picturesque fishing town, with several boats available for charter. A small park and picnic area have been developed at the end of Gogebic County Road 513.

[4]   Along the Black River Harbor road is the Copper Peak Ski Flying Hill, the highest artificial slide in the world. The International Ski Flying Tournament is held here each year in early March; competitors soar more than 500 feet in one of the most dramatic winter sports events. The present facility was built in 1969, although the peak was used for ski flying for decades before that. A chairlift and elevator to the top of the peak operate from May through October, daily, 9:00 to 5:00. The view over the adjacent forest and lake is magnificent. There is a charge.

[5]   Porcupine Mountains is the largest wilderness area under state control in Michigan, a lovely 58,000-acre region of lakes and hilly forest. There are eighty miles of hiking trails in the park, leading to a system of cabins, shelters, and campgrounds

scattered throughout the area. Cabins, containing four bunks, bedding, cooking utensils, wood stoves and a few tools must be reserved in advance. The shelters contain only bunks. There are 183 campsites, including two grounds right on the lakeshore: Union Bay at the park's eastern boundary, and Presque Isle River on the west. It is not possible to make a complete circuit of the park by car because most of the park's western area has been kept in a wilderness mode. There is a scenic drive from the eastern entrance, sixteen miles west of Ontonagon on State Highways 64 and 107, that leads to a viewpoint above Lake of the Clouds, cradled in the hills about 1,500 feet above sea level. Another forest road also skirts the southern boundary of the park.

[6]   The twin cities of Hancock and Houghton, built opposite each other along the hills above Portage Lake, were developed by a pair of brothers-in-law who arrived in the area seeking their fortunes in copper in the late 1840s. Ransom Shelden and Christopher Columbus Douglass discovered the Pewabic Lode and the Quincy Mine (see Copper Ghosts, this chapter). They then turned their attention to platting a pair of towns below the hill on which the mine was located. The towns were joined by a bridge in 1872. The next year a canal was completed across the lake at the base of the Keweenaw Peninsula, making the two towns a major port of the copper trade. Today the biggest activity in the area centers around Michigan Technological University in Houghton, founded in 1885 as a mining institution for the copper industry. The campus, in the eastern part of town on U.S. 41, houses the A. E. Seaman mineralogical collection, one of the best in the country, in the Electrical Engineering Building. It is open Monday to Friday, 9:00 to 4:30. There is no admission charge.

[7]   As U.S. 41 climbs Quincy Hill above Hancock, an overlook takes in both of the towns and the canal. The Quincy Lookout is a fitting introduction to the beauties of the Keweenaw.

[8]   Besides the Adventure Copper Mine, mentioned in Ghost Towns, this chapter, two other Copper Country mines offer daily tours. The Arcadian Mine in Ripley, east of Hancock on Michigan Highway 26, operates from June to mid-October, 8:00 to 4:30; in July and August it is open to 5:30. In Delaware,

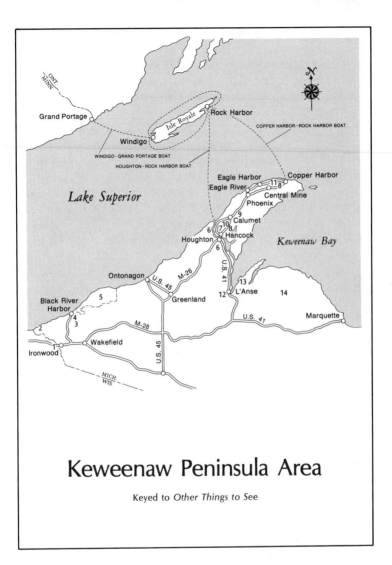

Keweenaw Peninsula Area

Keyed to *Other Things to See*

thirty-four miles northeast of Hancock on U.S. 41, the ancient Delaware Mine, one of the first in the area, is open daily, 10:00 to 6:00, June through September. There are admission charges in both mines.

[9]   Lake Linden was once the site of the central milling operations of the vast Calumet and Hecla Mines. Since 1962, the main office has been the Houghton County Historical Museum, an especially good exhibition center of what life was like on the northern frontier during the copper boom. The twenty-room facility is open daily, May 1 to October 1. There is an admission charge. Surrounding the museum building itself are the remains of the C&H milling operations. A self-guided tour may be taken of the exterior.

[10]   Laurium was one of the many communities that sprang up around the Calumet and Hecla mine works. Although not as atmospheric a place as neighboring Calumet, it does have its corner in history. At the entrance to the town on Michigan Highway 26 is the memorial to George Gipp, the Notre Dame football star of the World War I era, for whom later Irish teams were implored to go out and win one. Gipp was born in Laurium and is buried in the town cemetery.

[11]   Almost any Keweenaw County road is a scenic drive, but the best one is probably Michigan Highway 26 along the western shore between Phoenix and Copper Harbor. It runs along the coast, through the scenic county seat at Eagle River and the resort town of Eagle Harbor, past dazzling Lake Superior scenery.

[12]   For ten years, Fr. Frederic Baraga worked at L'Anse, making his mission there the center of his work among the Chippewa of Michigan, Minnesota, and Wisconsin. He began his work in North America at Madeline Island, moving to L'Anse in 1843 and remaining there until he was consecrated as the first Bishop of Upper Michigan. The shrine to this "snowshoe priest" rises on a bluff just north of L'Anse on U.S. 41. There is a thirty-five-foot high statue of the bishop holding a pair of snowshoes and a cross. The five wooden beams that support the brass monument symbolize his five major missions. A meditation area is adjacent to the statue. There is no admission charge.

[13]   In 1923 Henry Ford was searching for an Upper Peninsula port to handle his lumber and iron mining interests in the area. He settled upon Pequaming, on the eastern end of Keweenaw Bay, a few miles from L'Anse. Today it is an intriguing ghost town, with towering ruins of the old Ford works visible from across the bay. There are also abandoned homes and community buildings on the site and docks slowly rotting away—a haven for ghost town fanciers.

[14]   Somewhere east of L'Anse in Baraga County is Mt. Curwood, a peak of the Huron Range. At 1,980 feet, it is the highest point in Michigan. Situated as it is in a near wilderness amid dozens of similar peaks, it is quite difficult to find. If you're thinking of climbing it, the toughest part of the trip will be locating it. A good guide will help.

State Parks on the Lake

Porcupine Mountains is described in Other Things to See.

F. J. McLain, 9 miles west of Hancock on Michigan Highway 203, is a 401-acre facility with frontage on both Lake Superior and Bear Lake. There are hiking trails, a beach, a store, and picnic facilities. The park contains 90 campsites.

Fort Wilkins, 1 mile east of Copper Harbor, is described in the Copper Harbor section of this chapter. There are, in addition to the restored fort, boating and fishing facilities, hiking trails, and 163 campsites.

Baraga, 3 miles west of L'Anse on U.S. 41, is a 39-acre installation on Keweenaw Bay with swimming, fishing, and hiking. There are 137 campsites.

In Baraga State Forest is the remote Big Erics Bridge Campground. It is located 6 miles east of Skanee, which in turn is 20 miles northeast of L'Anse. It is in rugged Huron Mountain country, but its 20 campsites are just right for those who want solitude.

A ski flier challenges the 280-foot-high run at Ishpeming, Michigan. *Photo by Tom Buchkoe.*

Vein of Iron

On a blustery November day in 1844, William Burt's compass went wild on a hill in a remote corner of northern Michigan. One hundred miles to the northwest, the great copper rush had begun. Prospectors had come swarming up through the Soo to Copper Harbor and fanned out over the Keweenaw Peninsula to hunt for the metal. The Cliff Mine had been discovered earlier in the year, and the Fort Wilkins garrison had landed. Burt knew of all this, but it wasn't his concern. He was a surveyor and an already noted inventor, and his job was the running of government survey lines through this mostly unexplored part of Michigan. When his compass began fluctuating crazily, Burt took out one of his inventions, a solar compass, to gauge the direction of true north. He found the magnetic compass was being deflected by as much as 87 degrees. Burt scowled and looked around for axes. Whenever this had happened before it was because a member of his party had come too close to the compass with an ax blade. There was none near him now, though. Burt had a second idea and told the other surveyors to look around in the area for surface iron deposits. They kicked around in the pine roots and in a matter of minutes found a metal that looked very much like iron. Burt was elated, but not because of the iron. His solar compass had proven trustworthy, and in his mind that was the most significant event of the day. Burt reassembled his party and proceeded with the surveying job. From all appearances, he never gave the iron a second thought.

There were those who did, however. America in the 1840s was quite similar to current times in regard to its need to find more natural resources. Iron, especially, was becoming scarce. The great mills of Pennsylvania and Ohio already were in place, but the known deposits of the metal in the United States were running low. There were fears of an economic setback unless new sources could be found. Consequently, when news of Burt's find trickled down from the north, the excitement was huge and immediate.

One of the first men to reach the area was Philo Everett, of Jackson, Michigan. He was already in the vicinity searching for copper when he heard about the find. The following spring he engaged an Indian guide, Marji-Gesick, to lead him to the spot. The local tribes regarded the mountain to be haunted, and the guide only took him as far as its base. That was enough. Everett quickly ascertained the richness of the find. He called the place Jackson Mountain, after his hometown, then hastened off to file a claim. Before long, Michigan was going through its second mining rush in four years. The Upper Peninsula, which had seemed so barren and worthless when it was foisted upon the reluctant state only nine years before, was proving to be a treasure house.

The town of Negaunee grew up around the various diggings of the Jackson Iron Company. The city's official seal still depicts an uprooted pine tree, symbolizing how the initial find was made by the Burt party. A few miles to the west, the great Cleveland Mine developed. The melodiously named city of Ishpeming became centered around this mine which eventually made its owner, the Cleveland-Cliffs Company, the dominant firm on the iron range. Ishpeming, by the way, is an Ojibwa word meaning "high place" (the range on which it is situated is the watershed between Lakes Superior and Michigan). Perhaps as a tribute to the origin of its name, the city has erected a statue of an Indian brave in the main square. The statue is known affectionately as "Old Ish."

Later iron strikes were made in the Gogebic Range around Ironwood in the west and on the Menominee Range around Iron Mountain in the south, but the Marquette Range remained the most significant. As in the Copper Country, the iron range attracted great numbers of Cornish and Finnish immigrant miners, and the area still bears the imprint of their character. The Cornish influence is probably a bit stronger in this area.

As in the copper country, a big city grew up as a result of the mines. The port of Marquette began its life in 1849 as a post office on the part of Lake Superior nearest to the mines. The town was platted in 1854, the same year that the first ore dock was finished. A plank road was built between the mines and the port, and with the completion of the canal at Sault Ste. Marie, the place began to grow rapidly. But what was really needed was a railroad. The prospective builders of the line, however, were having trouble getting land acquisition rights from the state legislature in far-off Lansing. A local hero, Peter White, was elected to the legislature to help solve the problem. White had become a Marquette favorite by carrying mail between Green Bay and the isolated outpost during winter by strapping sacks across his back and setting out on snowshoes. He applied the same approach to representative government. White tramped most of the way to Lansing on his snowshoes. His arrival caused a sensation in the state capital, which was quite prepared to believe that Marquette was a howling wilderness populated exclusively by semi-savages. But White also proved to be an astute politician in the devious nineteenth-century manner; by 1857 Marquette had its railroad, bringing in 1,000 tons of ore daily.

The city never grew as big as Calumet in the copper district, but it proved far more stable. It is now the largest city in the Upper Peninsula, with about 25,000 residents, and is the cultural, commercial, and medical center for the region. Northern Michigan University has developed into a major state institution since its beginnings as tiny Northern Normal in 1889. Nearby K. I. Sawyer Air Force Base is a vital element in the city's economy, which has become increasingly diversified as the iron gives out.

Cleveland-Cliffs began experimenting with the pelletizing of low-grade ores to meet the standards of steel mills in 1959. Its Mather Mine was gradually expanded to become the largest underground operation in the world. But in 1978 the company announced that the mine would close, marking an end to deep-shaft operations in Michigan. Only surface, open-pit mining remains on the Marquette Range, but Michigan's vein of iron is still holding out.

Wind and water have carved natural sculptures at Michigan's Pictured Rocks National Lakeshore. *Photo by Bert Emanuele, courtesy of* Michigan Living/AAA Motor News.

Pictured Rocks National Lakeshore—West

Long before anyone came up with the idea of a national lakeshore, the Pictured Rocks were protected ground for the Chippewa. They believed that the gods lived there and that many of them flew above the crags in the form of eagles. Each summer, the Chippewa made their camp in the sheltered bay at Munising, just to the west of the rocks, and hunted and planted there. Many of the Hiawatha legends, spun into poetry two centuries later by Henry Wadsworth Longfellow, were set in this area. (It was at this place that Hiawatha was instructed in the arts of woodcraft and canoeing by the Daughter of the Moon, Nokomis.) At the annual midsummer festival, men of the tribe would hold a regatta along the massive rocks. They would throw tobacco and food into the water as offerings, and would have elaborate ceremonies to assuage any evil spirits who might inhabit the area.

The first European to visit the place, Pierre Radisson, observed the ceremonies in 1658 and came away impressed by the size of the rocks. Radisson must have gone by on a cloudy day, because it was not until years later that other explorers remarked on their vivid coloration. To the French the area was known as the Grand Portal, after one formation that rises 200 feet above the lake and seems to present a gigantic entryway to this twenty-two-mile stretch of shoreline. Only when an American expedition, led by Lewis Cass, came by after the War of 1812 did the name Pictured Rocks become attached to the place.

Thirty-eight miles of Lake Superior shore in this area, between Munising and Grand Marais, has been a national lakeshore since 1966. In all, it encompasses 67,000 acres. The coast is so varied, however, that it divides neatly into two sections. The first, or Pictured Rocks proper, is best seen from Munising. The second, described in the next section of this chapter, takes in the dunes and beaches of the Sable Banks. Grand Marais makes the best center for seeing this eastern part of the Lakeshore.

Munising occupies one of the loveliest settings on the Lakes. It is rimmed on three sides by green hills. A series of waterfalls come cascading down from the heights, many of them within the city limits. In the center of its bay is Grand Island, or in the Chippewa language, Menesing. The name was eventually altered slightly and given to the mainland settlement. Munising began as an iron furnace, one of several that local entrepreneurs tried to start up near the Marquette Range. Transportation and food expenses were so high at these sites, though, that they could not compete in price with the Lake Erie mills. By 1877, Munising's furnace, like most of the others, had gone out of operation. The town hung on long enough, however, to catch the start of the lumbering boom. A sawmill was established in 1895, and two years later Munising was incorporated as a town. The mill remains the major employer in the modern city of 3,500 people. The impressive sandstone Alger County Courthouse anchors one end of the main thoroughfare, Elm Avenue. At the other is the city dock, departure point for the Pictured Rocks cruises, the town's other leading industry.

Pictured Rocks Cruises, Inc., operates three boats that make the thirty-seven-mile round trip along the spectacular coastline from mid-June to mid-October. The trips take between two and a half and three hours, depending on water conditions. In July and August, cruises leave every other hour from 9:00 to 5:00. There are two daily cruises in the last two weeks of June and the first three weeks of September. During the fall color season, one daily trip leaves at 1:00. Reservations are advised. The phone number is 906-387-2379.

The boats leave the 229-foot-deep harbor, glide past the Grand Island light, and head out into the open lake. The first formation, Miners Castle, is also the only part of the Pictured Rocks that is accessible by car. County Road H-58, running east from downtown Munising, links up with County Road 13 to reach the Castle. It is approximately a twelve-mile drive. Beyond that, there is a hiking trail that runs the entire length of the Lakeshore. While this may be dandy exercise and a fine backpacking trip, there is really no way to appreciate the size and colors of the rocks except from the water.

Miners Castle supposedly was the site of a sermon delivered by Fr. Jacques Marquette to the Chippewa in 1668. It is fairly well established that the Jesuit explorer, then based at Sault Ste.

Marie, did visit the Indian summer encampment that year; whether he actually used this rock for a pulpit is unproven. It does make a nice image: the missionary standing on the rock, ninety feet above the lake, with his congregation bobbing around him in canoes.

The cruise continues past waterfalls that plummet over the rocks into the lake, small beaches tucked in between the cliffs, and, finally, the peak color areas. The rock here is ancient Cambrian sandstone underlain with minerals that oxidize as they come into contact with the air. The wind and waves of countless centuries have shaped the soft stone into fantastic formations, while seepage of the underlying minerals accounts for the brilliant coloration. The Indians had their own explanation. They saw the bright red rocks of one cave and concluded that barbarous rulers had left prisoners here to be dashed to pieces. They called it the Cave of the Bloody Chiefs.

The cruise goes on past rocks that resemble an Indian in profile, rocks that are used as an enormous rookery by gulls, rocks shaped like a battleship, a drum, a vase, and a solitary rock topped by a lone white pine. Along the way is the Portal, the massive formation that so impressed Radisson. If the water is calm, the boat can be maneuvered into a cove formed by a cleft in the rock. It is here, in a 200-passenger boat dwarfed by the towering cliffs, that you can fully appreciate the awesome scale of this coastline. It is a high point of any Great Lakes experience.

The cruise is accompanied by adept and informed commentary from the ship's captain. Once back on shore, take in some of Munising's waterfalls before leaving town. There are six of them within eight miles of downtown. Munising Falls, on County Road 58 in the eastern part of town, may be the prettiest, a fifty-foot drop into a natural amphitheater. Most impressive is Miners Falls, a seventy-five-foot torrent that carries more water than any other waterfall in the area. It is on the Miners Castle road, eight miles from Munising. There is no charge for viewing either falls.

Pictured Rocks National Lakeshore—East

Grand Marais is a resourceful little place. It has been pronounced dead any number of times, economically defunct and finished, yet it continues to hang on to delight the traveler who finds his or her way there from the main road. It is the eastern terminus of Pictured Rocks National Lakeshore and the starting point for trips to the Grand Sable Dunes to the west and to the wilderness of the Big Two-Hearted River country to the east. It offers, as much as any place on the Lakes, a world's-end ambience, too. The Mackinac Bridge is only 107 miles away. It seems much, much farther. The big lake slaps in on rocky beaches, and as night closes in the warning signal in the harbor is the only sound— other than an occasional click of a cue ball and a burst of laughter from the Skipper's Cove on the main street.

Grand Marais's population hovers around the 400 mark, maybe double that in the peak of the summer season when cottages are open. At one time it had a population of 2,500 and was one of the Upper Peninsula's livelier lumber towns. Its harbor, the only one between Munising and the Soo, was discovered by Pierre Radisson on his voyage of 1658. It became a regular stopover for voyageurs, and for many years a small fur trading post was situated there. It wasn't until the late 1870s, though, that permanent residents moved in. By 1882, it was a busy little lumbering town, a boom that lasted until the most accessible pine gave out in about eight years. That's when Grand Marais was given up for dead the first time. Its population fell to 200.

In 1893 the lumbermen returned, looking for hardwood and more remote pine stands. The Manistique Railroad was extended up from Seney (see chap. 6), and the village entered its most prosperous era. It had sixty-five business places on its streets. There were several elaborate hotels and saloons, two weekly newspapers, Saulson's Department Store, a cigar factory, and a telephone exchange. Then it all ended. There had been increasingly less work for the sawmills, and the railroad abruptly announced that it was closing down the spur on November 1, 1910. When the last train pulled out, a good part of Grand Marais's population pulled out with it. The town complained to both Washington and Lansing, but was told there was no way to keep the Manistique running. The town was isolated again. Two years later, the railroad came back and tore up the track for good measure. By that time only a shadow remained of Grand Marais.

By the mid 1920s, all that was left was a small fishing fleet (which would also be eradicated by the effects of the lamprey eel by 1962). The town was definitely finished. Visitors reported that grass was growing in the streets, buildings were falling to ruin, and birds were nesting in the chimneys of deserted houses. The visitors also said that they liked the place. The scenery was splendid, and there was all the serenity one could ever hope for. A few of the old homes were converted to summer places. In 1925, a blacktop road was built from Seney, paralleling the route of the old Manistique tracks. That opened the town up to a small-scale tourist trade. Over the last half-century, development hasn't gone much farther than that. The highway to Seney remains the only paved road into town. There are just two motels of any size (for a total of thirty-five rooms) and a civic campground on the lake. There are two waterfront parks that face in opposite directions—Bay Shore to catch the sunrise over the harbor and Woodland to watch it set into the lake. The onetime Saulson's Department Store is now a restaurant. A few other vintage operations have gone back into business. Tourism certainly hasn't brought the boom days back to Grand Marais; on the other hand, the town is not defunct.

The most popular excursion from town is west along County Road H-58. You can follow this road for about fifty miles all the way to Munising. Only one-third of it is paved, and the going can be rough in wet weather. The road goes through some wonderful stretches of white birch forests in the interior, but most of the big attractions are within fifteen miles of Grand Marais.

Just west of town is Sable Falls, a little gem of a cascade. It sprays down mistily over a series of rock terraces in a secluded wooded setting. One mile beyond the falls is the start of the dune country. Grand Sable Lake, a section of Superior cut off from the main body by acres of sand, has a small beach at the base of the dunes. Swimming here is a bit more comfortable than in the frigid waters of the big lake. In five more miles the road approaches the Grand Sable Banks, dunes towering right above Superior. Some of them are 275 feet above the water at a thirty-five-degree angle of incline. The banks are part of a glacial deposit. Over the centuries, vast accumulations of wind-blown sand created these mountainous dunes. The dunes are only half as high as the biggest in Sleeping Bear National Lakeshore on Lake Michigan in the Lower Peninsula. Nonetheless, in this much less crowded setting they make an impressive sight. The Banks run along the coast for five miles. One of their best-known features is the Devil's Slide, a natural chute from the top of the dune to the beach below. You can tumble all the way down, but you are then faced with the troublesome proposition of climbing back up again.

Immediately to the west of the slide is the Hurricane River Campground with eight primitive tent sites. From there it is a short walk to the abandoned but majestic Au Sable Light, now being restored by the National Park Service. Five miles further on the road is 12-Mile Beach Campground and eighteen more tent sites. This is a broad, almost untouched stretch of sand beach. All but the hardiest will eschew a quick dip in Superior's chilly waters, though.

The National Ski Hall of Fame

Among the popular sports, skiing is the unchallenged leader in glamour and economic clout. The wealthy build six-figure condominiums in the Colorado mountains, and the towns of Aspen and Vail probably have the highest per capita income in the country during high season. Sun Valley, Idaho, has become the epitome of wintertime luxury; the prestigious Olympic Games have been held in Squaw Valley, California, and Lake Placid, New York. The sport's pocketbook may be in these places, but its heart remains in tiny Ishpeming, an unglamorous iron-mining town without a French restaurant, Rolls-Royce, or high-rise condominium to its name.

The National Ski Hall of Fame has been located in Ishpeming since 1954, when it opened to commemorate the fiftieth anniversary of the United States Ski Association. This is where the Association was organized in the sport's Pleistocene Era, and this is where its officers felt the hall should be. In recent years, there has been some opposition to this idea. The new, monied interests that the sport has attracted have lobbied strongly for its transfer to a more accessible spot—preferably Denver or Squaw Valley. Association veterans will not hear of it, believing that history merits equal consideration with convenience. Besides, it is something of an American tradition to place athletic museums in rather remote locations. The best example is baseball's in Cooperstown, New York (a lovely village far from anything that resembles an Interstate, airport, or railroad depot). Basketball has placed its hall in Springfield, Massachusetts, and pro football in Canton, Ohio—both fair-sized cities but not exactly the crossroads of America. None, however, is quite as remote as Ishpeming.

It was here that skiing enjoyed its first great popularity in North America. When the iron mines of the Marquette Range opened, company recruiters were sent through northern Europe to find potential miners who were used to cold climates. Their most fertile territory was Norway and Finland. The iron country became heavily Scandinavian in the 1880s. Among the things the new immigrants brought with them was a love of skiing.

It was a far different kind of skiing from the sport that eventually swept the country. This skiing was limited to cross-country and to ski-flying, a heartstopping form of competition that involves soaring through the air after a lightning run down a high, steep slide. In modern times, ski fliers have gone almost 300 feet on the run at Ishpeming, which towers 280 feet above the valley and is known, aptly enough, as Suicide Hill. When Ishpeming's Norden Ski Club organized its first tournament in 1887, though, a jump of 50 feet was more than enough to win the event. Downhill racing, the mainstay of the sport today, did not come into vogue in America until the 1930s when instructors imported it from Switzerland and Austria. Ski-flying remains popular in the Scandinavian countries, Japan, and the Great Lakes area of the United States.

Carl Tellefsen arrived in Ishpeming to work in a bank in 1888, too late to register for the second tournament. He jumped anyhow, and his mark of 42.5 feet was greeted with acclaim. He had been a well-known jumper in his hometown of Trondheim, Norway, and by 1891 had become a leader of the local ski club. The sport was becoming popular throughout the northern Great Lakes. There are other areas of the country that have strong historical claims antedating the development of skiing here, but nowhere else was it as well-organized or attended. A group of eleven ski clubs met in Ishpeming to form a regional association, regarded as a forerunner of the United States Ski Association. It disbanded, but Tellefsen was convinced that the sport required organization at the national level. In 1904 he finally put together a national tournament which, of course, called for a national regulating body. Crowds estimated as high as 10,000 arrived in Ishpeming by special trains to watch the contest, and the new Association was off to an impressive start. The offices eventually moved to Denver, but the hall of fame remains here.

For years, the hall was hindered by lack of funds. Unlike other popular sports, there is no professional league to underwrite the costs of the museum. The hall has scraped by on individual donations. (For a while it was in the anomalous position of having to shut down in winter, during the height of the ski season.) Some recent grant money, most notably from the

Cleveland-Cliffs mining company, has enabled it to expand and modernize its exhibits and to lengthen its hours of opening. The hall is now open daily, 10:00 to 4:00, mid-June to Labor Day; Wednesday to Sunday, 1:00 to 4:00, for the rest of the year. A donation is asked.

The two-story museum building is located on Mather Avenue in a residential area, but the route to it from U.S. 41 is well marked. On the ground floor are historical displays tracing the evolution of the sport from its 4,000-year-old roots to the present. There is special attention paid to Scandinavian and local antecedents, including a special exhibit case devoted to the Bietela brothers. Two of the Bietelas are enshrined in the hall, and the ski-jumping tournament at Suicide Hill held each February is named for Paul Bietela, who was killed at the age of twenty in a tournament at St. Paul. There are also more than enough exhibits especially interesting to downhill skiers. On the second floor are the plaques honoring the great names of skiing—from Tellefsen to Billy Kidd to Bud Werner to Jill Kinmount. They are names that even the Aspen aprés-ski crowd would know.

Other Things to See

[1]   Open-pit mining operations are all that remain on the Marquette Iron Range. One of the biggest is the Republic Mine, off Michigan Highway 95, about eight miles south of U.S. 41. There is an observation platform at the mine to permit sidewalk superintendents to have a field day.

[2]   The beginnings of iron mining in Michigan are commemorated with a monument in Jackson Park, on U.S. 41 in Negaunee. A pyramid of iron ore marks the approximate spot at which the vein was accidentally discovered in 1844 by William Burt's surveying party. Nearby is the Jackson Mine Museum, containing memorabilia from this pioneer iron operation. Hours vary, and it is best to check locally.

[3]   Big Bay is another remote Lake Superior town that has been discovered by a small number of travelers who like to get away. The Big Bay Hotel, built by Henry Ford just before World War II, was reopened in 1977 after a hiatus of ten years. Many of the scenes from the motion picture *Anatomy of a Murder,* set in the Upper Peninsula, were filmed here.

[4]   Marquette may be the biggest city in the Upper Peninsula, but drive for a few minutes north of town and you are deep in a near wilderness. The Marquette and Huron Mountain Railroad makes fifteen-mile excursions along this part of the lakeshore from its depot on Lake Shore Boulevard near Presque Isle Park. The trips, aboard a 1910 steam train, depart daily at 9:30 and 2:00, from mid-June to Labor Day. In the last weekend of September and the first two weekends of October, the train leaves at 12:30 only. Breakfast is served on the morning runs at an extra charge of $2.50.

[5]   Marquette's playground is Presque Isle Park, a stunning 328-acre peninsula that juts into Lake Superior at the northern end of the city. There is a small zoo there along with beaches, picnic grounds, boat ramps, and full recreational facilities. A one-way drive makes a circuit of the area and leads to fine viewpoints over the lake.

[6]   When the big lake freighters pull up to the ore docks to

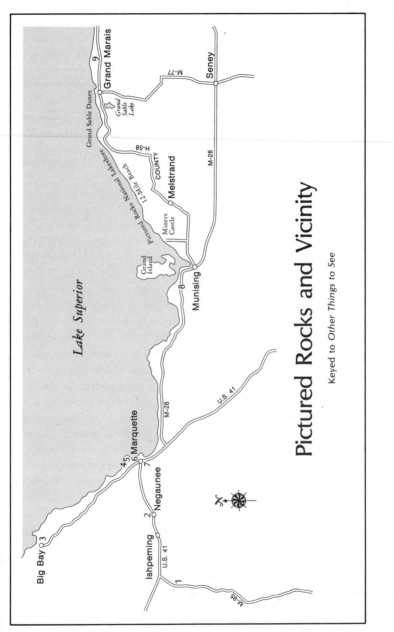

Pictured Rocks and Vicinity

Keyed to Other Things to See

receive their loads, it is an irresistible sight to both visitors and natives of Marquette. There are two places in the city to watch the process. The Lake Superior and Ishpeming Railroad docks are just south of Presque Isle on Lake Shore Boulevard. The Soo Line docks are located downtown, and there are views of them from adjacent docks and from Lakeside Park (also noted for its 1897 sculpture of Father Marquette.) Since the docks ship out about seven million tons annually, your chances of seeing the operation are quite good.

[7]   The Marquette County Historical Museum gives a fairly good picture of the area's colorful iron-mining and lumbering past. The museum is located at 213 North Front Street and is open daily, 9:00 to noon and 1:00 to 4:30. A donation is asked. Another look at the city's proud past can be seen one block north by walking east on Arch Street. Between Front Street and Lake Shore Boulevard this street is lined with some of the most interesting late Victorian homes in the city, with many variations in style. The museum also operates the John Burt House, a restoration of the city's first house, built in 1858. It is located in the southern part of the city, at 200 Craig Street, three blocks west of U.S. 41 on Genesee Street, then two blocks south. It is open daily, 9:00 to 5:00, in July and August. A donation is asked.

[8]   Bay Furnace was among the first communities that had their beginnings as iron mills near the Marquette Range. It was more successful than most, producing 38,000 tons of pig iron between 1869 and 1875. In 1876 the town burned down and was never rebuilt. The ruins of the old furnace, now situated in Hiawatha National Forest, are maintained just west of the town of Christmas on Michigan Highway 28.

[9]   The road running east of Grand Marais looks substantial enough on the map, but it soon turns into an unpaved track heading into one of Michigan's most extensive wilderness countries. Ernest Hemingway wrote about the Big Two-Hearted River, and the area is almost as it was when he fished it in the years after World War I. It is an area in which snowmobilers get lost every winter and hikers every summer, and a reminder that the Upper Peninsula, Mackinac Bridge or no, is still a big and wild place.

Side Trip

Forest Road 13, running through the western part of Hiawatha National Forest, is regarded as one of the best scenic drives in the area. It runs from Wetmore to Nahma Junction through an area of birch forests and lakes, with barely a commercial interruption on the way.

State Parks on the Lake

There is camping at Bay Furnace (see Other Things to See), 5 miles west of Munising, in Hiawatha National Forest. There are 50 campsites in the area. Nearby in the National Forest is Au Train Lake Campground, 7 miles southeast of Au Train on forest roads, with 36 campsites.

A series of campgrounds are located along County Road H-58 as it runs south of the Pictured Rocks National Lakeshore between Munising and Grand Marais. They are, west to east, North Gemini Lake (18 sites), South Gemini Lake (5 sites), Ross Lake (10 sites), and Kingston Lake (14 sites). They all lie between 10 and 16 miles east of Melstrand, the point at which the paved portion of the road ends.

Muskallonge Lake State Park, 27 miles north of Newberry on Michigan Highway 123 and County Road 37, lies in a Lake Superior wilderness. The lakeshore is good hunting grounds for rockhounds, and there are hiking and boating facilities. The park has 179 campsites.

Seney Wildlife Refuge provides a haven for Canada geese and many other migratory birds. *Courtesy Michigan Travel Commission.*

Lake Michigan's Northern Shore

It is a long and haunted shore. In 150 miles, between the Mackinac Bridge and Escanaba, you will pass only one town of any size: Manistique. But you will be inundated by ghosts: lumbering camps, railroad towns, fishing ports. Groscap, Brevort, Epoufette—the road map dutifully lists them, although all that remains may be a filling station and a store. The trees have been harvested, the fish have been caught, and the railroad doesn't stop here anymore. All that breaks the stillness is U.S. 2 making its solitary run across the forest along the northern coast of Lake Michigan.

Most of this shoreline is public land, the Hiawatha National Forest and the Mackinac State Forest. Cut over once, the land was abandoned, and it reverted to the government. Now it is productive—the stands of pine that once supported entire towns again spread across the land—and serves an additional function as recreation grounds.

The towns the forest sheltered used to be substantial places, some with more than 1,000 inhabitants. Nahma's sawmills were capable of a daily production of 100,000 board feet of lumber. Now its shuttered buildings house a tiny remnant of the thriving town that was. Brevort once stretched for two miles along the lakefront. In the 1880s Naubinway had a fishing fleet of thirty-four boats taking thousands of tons of whitefish and trout from the lake. The catch was so huge and seemingly inexhaustible that sturgeon were cast away as waste. It was a kill fully as efficient as the destruction of the bison on the western plains. By 1887, restrictive regulations had gone into effect, but the fishing industry never regained the importance it had in previous years. The towns that had served as its ports slowly faded away.

Fayette, on the Garden Peninsula, has become an institutionalized ghost town, a museum subsidized by the state of Michigan as a historic state park. However, dozens of other towns either have vanished altogether or linger on in a twilight world only as real as a dot on a road map. Even having a famous man as a namesake didn't help some places. Kipling, named by the general manager of the Soo Line railroad for his favorite writer, Rudyard Kipling, once lay north of Escanaba on Little Bay de Noc. A companion town named Rudyard was also chosen to honor the author. Kipling, much flattered, responded in verse:

Wise is the child who knows his sire,
The ancient proverb ran.
But wiser far the man who knows
How, when and where his offspring grows
For who the mischief would suppose
I've sons in Michigan.

Kipling's Michigan offspring didn't fare well, despite the rhyme. Rudyard is now a back road hamlet off Interstate 75, south of Sault Ste. Marie. Kipling, which once boasted a blast furnace, had dwindled to a population of twenty-five by the 1940 census, the last in which it appeared. Now it no longer formally exists, even on the maps.

The villages of Epoufette and Groscap, like many places on this shore, still bear their seventeenth-century French designations, indicating a paucity of subsequent American settlement. Epoufette means "resting place." It was supposed that Fr. Jacques Marquette put into its harbor on his first night out from St. Ignace during his voyage of discovery in the west. Seul Choix Point means "only choice," since it offered the only harbor in many miles for mariners caught in a storm. Point Aux Chenes refers to the oak trees on the headland, and Groscap calls attention to the elevation of the cape. Pointe La Barbe, the last cape before the Straits of Mackinac, means "the beard." Voyageurs returning to Mackinac from the west knew that when they saw this cape it was time to shave and prepare to return to civilization.

Schoolcraft County was named for a man who was quite a namer of things himself. Henry R. Schoolcraft, trained as a geologist, took part in a pioneer expedition to size up this northern wilderness for the U.S. government. He was enthralled by the Indians he encountered and decided to devote his life to learning their language and their lore. He was appointed Indian agent at Mackinac and the Soo. The material he gathered from area tribes eventually was woven into the epic *Song of Hiawatha* by his poet friend Henry Wadsworth Longfellow. When Michigan Territory was faced with the task of organizing and naming counties, it called on Schoolcraft to come up with appropriate Indian names. An incurable romantic, Schoolcraft produced a selection of mellifluous words, amalgamations of various tribal dialects and hybrids of Latin and Chippewa. They sounded authentic, and many of Michigan's Lower Peninsula counties still bear these concocted "Indian" names.

Delta County was given its name because its shape originally resembled a triangle (delta in Greek). Later territorial revisions changed the shape but not the name. Its seat, Escanaba, is the third largest city in the Upper Peninsula, the only ore-shipping port on Lake Michigan, and the site of the U.P.'s version of the state fair each August. South of Escanaba, the lakeshore again is an empty place, although the beaches in this area have given it a much livelier resort trade than on the northern coast.

The twin cities of Menominee, Michigan, and Marinette, Wisconsin, make up the largest center of population on the lake north of Green Bay. Separating the towns is the Menominee River, named for the wild rice that once grew in profusion in this area. The river, following a looping, meandering course, continues to mark the boundary line between the states as it goes through the near wilderness area northwest of the twin cities. It took a United States Supreme Court ruling in 1936 to settle this boundary, one hundred years after the Upper Peninsula was taken away from Wisconsin to satisfy Michigan for losing Toledo to Ohio.

Former lumbering towns that survived the transition of the area to agriculture—Peshtigo and Oconto—break up the last leg of the long journey to Green Bay.

Fayette

At the age of ninety-two Fayette officially became a ghost. Once a bustling smelting town in the pioneer days of the iron industry, it had stood empty and decaying since 1891, when the furnaces shut down and the workers went away. Changes in the method of iron production and in transportation made the place superfluous, and the Jackson Iron Company, which built it as a company town in 1867, decided to shut it down. Fayette lingered on for more than half a century, its buildings tumbling to ruin and its great furnaces looming like ossified dinosaurs above the waters of Snail Shell Harbor. Finally, in 1959, it was acquired by the state of Michigan and turned into a museum. Although a ghost town, Fayette now is livelier than at any time since the height of its prosperity.

When iron ore was discovered near Negaunee in 1845, the Jackson Iron Company was organized to exploit the valuable new lode. In those days, however, the Upper Peninsula of Michigan was far more remote from the rest of the nation than it is today. New York editor Horace Greeley, writing at about that time, described the U.P. as "cold and uninviting to the cultivator, diversified by vast swamps, sterile gravelly knolls and dense forests." To the America of that era, it was as distant and forbidding as Patagonia. There was no canal at Sault Ste. Marie, and transportation costs back to the east were prohibitive. Shipping crude ore, which contained about 40 percent waste, was an inefficient proposition at costs of eight dollars a ton. Fayette Brown, general manager of the Jackson Iron Company, determined that a better idea would be to smelt the ore in the Upper Peninsula and then send only the pig iron south, reducing transportation costs considerably. He began looking for a site. It would require a natural harbor and large amounts of limestone and hardwood in the vicinity. (Limestone was needed for furnace flux to remove oxides from the ore; hardwood was used to provide charcoal that fueled the furnaces.) The company already had built a rail line from the mine to the Lake Michigan port of Escanaba, so the search for a smelting site was concentrated in the area within a reasonable distance of its docks. They found it on the Garden Peninsula, on the eastern shore of Big Bay de Noc. By 1866 the company had acquired 15,000 acres in the area, and began to put together the town that would be named after its general manager.

By May of 1867 the place had a blast furnace, ore docks, shops, offices, and accommodations for workers. Fayette had come to life. A second furnace was added in 1870, and three years later the town was producing 14,000 tons of pig iron annually. Even so, it handled only 20 percent of the company's smelting. Transportation costs had dipped to about three dollars a ton, and it was only marginally more expensive to ship the ore to the older smelting operations in Ohio and New York. Still, the company was able to operate Fayette at a profit. Blacksmith and carpentry shops were added. There were forty log houses and nine frame dwellings on the site, and a narrow-gauge railroad to bring in wood. The limestone came from giant cliffs that guarded the harbor entrance right outside of town.

Fayette reached its peak in 1884. That year it had a population of about 1,000 and produced 16,875 tons of ore. The valuation of the site was $300,000. The company made every effort to provide the amenities to everyone in Fayette, but social stratification was quite visible. At the top, in both the organization chart and his homesite, was the company superintendent. His house occupied the best spot in town—on the bluff overlooking the harbor—and he was, in every respect, the first citizen. Although his privy was located outside, it did have wallpaper and plaster. The company kept a resident physician at Fayette at all times; just a few yards down the street was his house, a comfortable two-story affair. Down the hill and closer to the center of town were the residences of the foremen and skilled tradesmen and their families, while the unskilled workers lived in simple log buildings. Rent was deducted by the company from monthly earnings. Since the company also owned the stores and all other services in town, these charges, too, were tallied up and came out of the worker's pay. By month's end, a worker might find all his needs nicely attended to but very little cash left over for his pockets.

Saloons and alcoholic beverages were prohibited in town,

Only skeletons remain of the iron works that made Fayette a bustling smelting town in the 1800s. *Courtesy the Detroit News.*

although when one long-time employee was disabled on the job the company magnanimously allowed him to open a tavern just outside the city limits. All in all, it was not an unpleasant place by the standards of the late nineteenth-century frontier. There was a two-story hotel that boasted hot running water and a privy attached by bridge to the main building. There was an opera house which was used for community gatherings, political assemblies, and performances by visiting theatrical troupes. There was an Odd Fellows chapter, a cornet band, a debating club, a school, and facilities for three religious groups—Catholic, Methodist, and Congregational. There was a town baseball team that toured the U.P. in summer, and a horse racing track (sponsored by superintendent Henry Merry). In winter, though, Fayette knew terrible isolation. Navigation on the bay was uncertain, and communication with the outside world could be cut off for weeks at a time. In 1876 a purse of $100 was offered to anyone making it to Escanaba and bringing back news of the presidential election. A daring traveler collected the reward, but all he could report was that the result was in dispute and had been put to the election commission.

Technological progress sealed Fayette's fate in the 1880s, when the coke blast furnace was developed as a less costly method of making pig iron. Area forests had been cut over, and it was becoming more expensive to bring charcoal fuel into Fayette. The town could no longer pay its way. In 1891 the company closed down the furnaces, moved the employees off the site, and sold the property to the Cleveland-Cliffs Company. In its twenty-four years of production, Fayette had turned out 229,268 tons of iron.

Cleveland-Cliffs held on to the site for twenty-five years, selling out to a pair of Wisconsin businessmen in 1916. Thirty years later it came into the hands of a Detroit woman who planned to turn it into a resort. Nothing came of that, though, and in 1956 Fayette was sold at auction to satisfy back taxes. Three years later the state swapped some land with the Mead Paper Company of Escanaba to acquire the site and turn Fayette into a historical state park.

Many of the buildings are undergoing restoration under the

careful supervision of historians. The ground floor of the opera house is now a small museum of daily life in Fayette. Several of the supervisors' homes have been returned to their furnished appearance of the 1880s. The doctor's house and machine shop also have been fully restored; work is proceeding on the hotel and superintendent's house. In addition, a modern interpretive museum and a scale model of Fayette as it looked in its prime are located in a visitor's center at the park entrance. The massive furnace complex, its roaring fires banked for nearly a century, still dominates the site. The stone ruins form a picturesque frame for the lovely harbor below. The historic buildings are open April through October, from 8:00 A.M. to 10:00 P.M. There is an admission charge. The park also contains eighty campsites and facilities for water sports, picnicking, and hiking.

Peshtigo

On a golden October day in 1871 the fire came by for Peshtigo. A tornado of flame sweeping up from the southwest devoured the entire city and more than 1,200 people in the immediate area. It was over in twenty minutes. The firestorm passed and left the lumbering town of Peshtigo in ashes. There had been nothing like it in history, and it was not to be repeated until the fire bombings of Tokyo and Dresden in World War II.

Yet until the early 1950s this terrible disaster, the greatest fire catastrophe in American experience, was all but forgotten. Lists of historic fires compiled before then invariably omitted the Peshtigo inferno. It happened that on the same Sunday evening that Peshtigo was destroyed, the Chicago fire was starting several hundred miles to the south. The spectacle of one of the country's greatest urban centers being leveled seemed to diminish the impact of any other disaster, no matter how horrible. Or perhaps the country was just numbed by the Chicago disaster and could absorb no more when news of Peshtigo got out. Hundreds died in the Chicago blaze, and the property loss was enormous, but there had been some warning, time to get out, and places to flee for safety. In Peshtigo there was no time and no refuge. The flames were upon its residents before they had time to move. Only those who made it to the Peshtigo River, and a few others spared by luck, survived.

It was not until eighty years later that the Peshtigo story was publicized. Except for a brief plea for assistance in the days immediately following the blaze, Peshtigo chose to bury the memory with the dead. While the Chicago fire passed into folklore, Peshtigo's was forgotten—except by those who had lived through it. The story was passed on and, as the original survivors died, retold at their funerals. As that select list dwindled to a handful in the early 1950s, Peshtigo decided that a more lasting memorial was necessary. In 1951 the town erected a monument at a mass grave of 350 unidentified victims. It compiled oral histories of remaining survivors. It established a museum in a former church building near the cemetery. And slowly the world began to realize the enormity of what had happened here so long ago.

Peshtigo in 1871 was a little boomtown of about 2,000 people. Logging operations were going on all around it. The lumber was seen as such an inexhaustible resource that smaller trees were simply abandoned where they fell so the giants could be harvested. Sawdust filled the streets of the town, and the sidewalks were made of pine. The largest woodenware factory in the world was the major employer. There were also rail crews in the area, extending the Chicago and Northwestern line to Menominee. As they cleared the right-of-way, large piles of debris were left to burn.

It had been a hot and unusually dry summer. There was barely a trace of rain after July, and autumn began the same way. In the surrounding swamps, peat fires began to burn, and nearby farmers lost their fields to the flames. They fled into town. Peshtigo residents had been called on periodically to beat out grass fires caused by sparks and embers from these surrounding blazes and the railroad debris. The morning of Sunday, October 8, was recalled as being unnaturally still. Smoke hung in the air from the nearby fires. The sky was a strange copper color throughout the day. At sunset it began to turn pink, and an eerie glow lit the west. The wind picked up and started to come from the southwest. Then the townspeople heard the roar.

"It was a seething, searing hell," said one survivor years later, "and the hurricane it was riding traveled almost as fast as light itself. It swept in so suddenly that no man could say for sure what happened in the next few minutes." A wall of flame had formed southwest of town and was advancing at the speed of a trotting man. Wildlife fled before it. Birds trying to fly away fell, scorched, to the ground. What Peshtigo had seen at sunset was the crown of the fire, burning across the top of the forest. A rain of ashes fell on the town. Balloons of flame made of gases sucked up from the swamps filled the air. The updraft of heat created a cyclone, a tornado of flame that shook the ground with its fury. Embers and sparks blew like a fiery blizzard. People gasped and clutched at their throats. The fire was sucking up oxygen, and many of the dead suffocated before being burned. The very air seemed to be ablaze. Then the inferno was upon them.

Seventy-five people ran for refuge in a boarding house and were consumed in a flash. Those who hesitated to watch the fire were turned instantly into pillars of flame. One family, trapped in its cabin, committed suicide by knife rather than wait for the flames. Others sought safety in wells, only to die of suffocation.

Those who could ran for the Peshtigo River bridge, only to meet crowds fleeing in panic from the opposite bank. The bridge collapsed under their weight, but the river was the only safe place anyway. One man was able to get his children to the water in a wheelbarrow but was roasted before he could plunge in himself. Even those standing in the water were killed by the superheated air if they failed to immerse themselves.

The fire raced on, burning down much of Menominee and destroying the entire village of Birch Run, Michigan, with its population of fifty. Observers seated on hillsides in Ironwood, Michigan, 200 miles away, reported they had seen the blaze. Sparks carried by the strong winds leaped across Lake Michigan and began to burn across the Lower Peninsula of Michigan. In the next few days the blaze would reach all the way to Lake Huron and beyond, consuming many towns in Michigan's Thumb before burning itself out near Chatham, Ontario.

A light rain began to fall in Peshtigo at dawn of October 9. A few men walked to Menominee to summon help. Rescuers came to Peshtigo and found only ashes. Ax blades marked the spot where twenty firefighters had been last seen digging trenches. In a hardware store, dozens of blades had fused into one giant sheet of metal. A few dozen survivors emerged from one house which had been built of green wood that did not ignite in the blaze. Others had escaped by digging holes and burying themselves. An infant was found at the side of the road. No one knew her name or family, so she was called Nettie Dutton and raised by survivors of the fire. She lived in Peshtigo for another eighty years. Her death was one of the events that renewed interest in the forgotten disaster so many years later.

The final toll was 1,182 dead. The city of Peshtigo had died, too, but like Chicago it was soon rebuilt. People picked up what they could and tried to forget, until it seemed somehow more important, years later, that the story be told. Today Peshtigo is a neat town of about 3,000 people. On Oconto Avenue, just off the business district, is the cemetery, with monuments and markers retelling the story of the fire. A few yards to the north is the Peshtigo Fire Museum. Because of the nature of the event, there is not really much that a museum can preserve. There are, however, artifacts of the period and a huge mural of the fire, as well as photographs and other displays relating to local history. The museum is open Memorial Day to the first weekend in October (the anniversary of the fire), daily, 9:00 to 5:00. A donation is asked.

Seney National Wildlife Refuge

There are some who would argue that Seney always has been a wildlife refuge. In its early days, though, the wildlife happened to be of the human variety. During the peak of the Upper Peninsula's lumbering era, in the 1880s and '90s, Seney wore the reputation as the toughest town in the north. It was said that if a man went to a railroad station and ordered a ticket to hell he'd be sent on the train to Seney. It was said that if the Detroit post office received a piece of undeliverable mail it would be forwarded to Seney on the good chance the intended recipient had joined the rollicking lumberjack crews. It was said that two lumberjacks with a feud of five years' standing met on Seney's main street and fought each other for a solid hour from one end of town to the other. Some of what was said might have even been true. That Seney, however, vanished long ago with the pine forests. A new breed of roughneck, the land swindler, then came upon the scene in the early 1900s. Several dozen unfortunates were bilked of their life's savings in a crack-brained scheme to turn the surrounding marshland into farms. By the 1930s, the forests and the marshes had been ravaged. The area was a mess, a wasteland of no use to anyone.

This is the land that became the Seney National Wildlife Refuge, a 95,000-acre tract that has become one of the most popular preserves in the federal system. Its chief attraction is the Canada geese and other migratory wildfowl that have established annual nesting grounds here in summer. There are also several species of duck, occasional bald eagles, sandhill cranes—over 200 species of birds may be seen here. There are guided tours, auto drives, and observation towers from which to do the viewing.

The refuge is located five miles south of the town of Seney, which sits at the intersection of Michigan Highways 28 and 77. In the previous century, the junction was a rail crossing, the transportation center of the lumbering industry. Founded in 1882, it had a peak population of 3,000, with six lumbering companies located in town and fifteen camps in the vicinity. Lumberjacks came in from the winter cutting season, paychecks in their pockets, eager to raise forty-six distinct varieties of hell. Within ten years of its birth Seney had a national reputation as a pit of vice, which must have been quite embarrassing for proper New Yorker George L. Seney, the railroad director for whom the town was named.

The reputation was probably merited. By some accounts, there were twenty-one saloons and as many houses of pleasure in town. At the spring breakup, every hustler in the north would gather there. There was P. J. ("Snap Jaw") Small, who engagingly bit the heads off live frogs and snakes to cadge drinks. There was "Protestant Bob" McGuire, noted for his eye-gouging techniques in fights. There was Dan Dunn, who shot one of the Harcourt boys and, while in police custody, was himself gunned down by another Harcourt. His killer served three years in prison and returned home to win election as a township supervisor.

Newspaperwoman Nellie Bly gave the town its greatest notoriety by reporting on "white slavery" stockades there, with fierce dogs trained to track down any unfortunate who tried to escape. The story was a hoax staged by local residents to enliven Miss Bly's stay in Seney. It was born of the same sense of fun that prompted Seney citizens to greet incoming trains and turn passengers upside down to collect their fallen change. They knew how to have a good time in Seney. After the Bly story was published, there were calls for a congressional investigation and demands to shut Seney down. But the end of the lumbering era accomplished that soon enough, and a forest fire finished the job in 1904. Seney became the tiny crossroads of a few hundred people that it is today, its wickedest diversion a pool table.

The short-lived development of New Seney came in 1911. This community was to be established south of town in the Great Manistique Swamp. The Western Land Securities Company of St. Paul, Minnesota, promoted the venture throughout the Midwest. There would be 4,450 farms on tracts of 160 acres apiece. Advertisements described parks and streets, a community of 50,000 settlers. The soil, said the ads, was "marsh prairie, with deposits of rich muck, several feet in depth. The low lands are easily drained. They are capable of producing very heavy crops of all kinds grown in a temperate climate for an almost indefinite period with fertilizers." The lure was taken. Eager buyers paid up to $17.50 an acre for almost worthless land in a climate that was "temperate" in comparison, perhaps, to Siberia but unfit for growing any substantial crops. Many potential farmers came from Minnesota, selling their homes to buy the land. A group of 150 blacks arrived from Illinois looking for a new life in the north. They lasted less than a year. A wealthy Chicago man actually tried to start a 3,000-acre sheep ranch. Most of his stock died of starvation during the winter, and the coyotes killed the rest. The developers brought in huge dredgers, hauled by teams of twenty-four horses, to attack the swamp. They went at it for two years, then gave up. The battered land was sold for taxes, and New Seney disappeared.

The land sat empty for twenty years. Then, during the Depression, the state turned it over to the federal government as a wildlife refuge. It became a project of the Civilian Conservation Corps of the New Deal, and young men from around the country came to Seney for work. They restored the marsh, built a system of dikes, ditches, water control mechanisms, and roads, and impounded 7,000 acres of water in twenty-one pools. A flock of captive Canada geese was donated to the new refuge in 1936. Within eight years they had attracted wild geese, and Seney had become a permanent stop on the summer migratory trail. A forest management program is going on at the refuge in an effort to bring back the trees and improve the habitat. There is even farming on 450 acres to raise supplemental food for the animals. There is limited fishing and hunting, too.

The refuge's visitor center is open daily, April through October. It provides orientation, dioramas, and environmental exhibits in a small museum building. Visitors can go out on their own, on a self-guided, seven-mile auto tour. It may be taken from 8:00 to 4:30, June 15 to Labor Day. The road winds slowly around the ponds, but during the midday hours it is difficult to spot wildlife. A guided tour at 6:00 P.M. is a better choice, if you have the time. It lasts for two hours and is offered from late June to September 15. There is no admission charge to the refuge or for the tour. There is also a nature trail that runs for slightly more than a mile from the visitor center to a 100-foot observation tower. The refuge is entered from Highway 77, between Seney and Germfask.

Other Things to See

[1]   Between St. Ignace and Naubinway, U.S. 2 is an especially scenic road, winding through forests that overlook the lake.
It passes through the Hiawatha National Forest as far as Brevort,
and from there it enters the Mackinac State Forest. At Point Aux
Chenes, between Groscap and Brevort, is a national forest visitor
information center and a nature walk into the adjacent marsh.
The national forest is a sprawling 863,000-acre preserve, established in 1931 to restore the pine and hardwood ravaged in the
lumbering era. It is divided into an eastern and western section;
in its entirety it extends the entire breadth of the Upper Peninsula, from Lake Michigan to Lake Superior. There are several
campgrounds in both the national and state forests. The state
forest extends along the shoreline for twenty miles and also em-
braces many inland lakes. It covers an area of 180,000 acres,
with headquarters in Naubinway.

[2]   Manistique is an old paper-milling town situated on a
lovely bay, but its biggest attraction is a bridge that is lower than
the water it crosses. The siphon bridge, which provides the
roadway for U.S. 2 across the Manistique River, was created by
the Manistique Pulp and Paper Company in 1916. Engineers
were faced with the need for building a dam that would not flood
portions of the city and could also be crossed inexpensively by
road. The solution they hit upon was building a concrete tank in
the river that provided an artificially higher shoreline for the
roadbed while damming the river waters. You really can't see the
effect from your car, but if you park at the far end and walk back
along the bridge you can watch the waters lapping above your
viewpoint.

[3]   The best time to visit Kitch-iti-pi is early in the morning, when the mist is rising from the water and the only sounds
are the calls of birds and the ripples made by trout in the pond.
This is the biggest spring in Michigan, so large that an entire state
park, Palms Book, was created as a setting. Water bubbles from
about twenty fissures in the limestone, over 10,000 gallons per
minute at a year-round temperature of forty-five degrees. It is 40
feet deep at its center and 200 feet wide. By means of self-

operated rafts, visitors can float to the middle of the spring. Through glass openings they can see moss-encrusted tree trunks, clouds of sand stirred up by the constantly moving water, and fish moving through the shadows. It is a glimpse of a fantasy world. Old legends tell of an Indian girl who leaped into the spring and was changed into a white deer (whose outline may still be discerned in the spring bottom by the imaginative). There is an entrance fee to the state park, but the raft trip is free. It does not operate during the winter months. Palms Book State Park is twelve miles northwest of Manistique along Michigan Highway 149.

[4]   Those with a taste (either sporting or culinary) for trout will want to visit the State Fish Hatchery at Thompson. It is dedicated to the raising of trout, and is the largest of its kind in the world. It is located just off U.S. 2, and is open daily from 8:00 to 4:30. There is no admission charge.

[5]   Ludington Park is Escanaba's opening on the lake, and the city has developed it as a spacious, attractive recreation grounds with all sorts of water and land-based sports facilities. The park's towering old oaks also shelter the Delta County Historical Museum, a collection of local history recalling Escanaba's days as a railhead and an ore-shipping port. It is open daily, 1:00 to 5:00, late May and June; 1:00 to 9:00 until Labor Day. Admission to the park is free. A donation is asked at the museum.

[6]   Menominee takes advantage of both its lakefront and its river in two first-rate city parks. Henes Park, donated to the city by a pioneer family in 1905, is in the northeastern corner of the city, off State Highway 35. Besides a beach and picnic grounds, there are also a small zoo and enclosures for deer, buffalo, and wildfowl. Stephenson Island is shared by Menominee and Marinette, Wisconsin, with the U.S. 41 bridge running right through it. There are attractive picnic areas along the Menominee River and local logging museum. The Henes Park Zoo is open daily, June to October, 6:00 A.M. to 11:00 P.M. There is no admission charge. The Stephenson Island Museum is open daily from late May to October, 10:00 to 5:00. There is an admission charge.

[7]   The brig *Alvin Clark* went to the bottom of Green Bay in a storm during 1864. She lay near Chambers Island for more

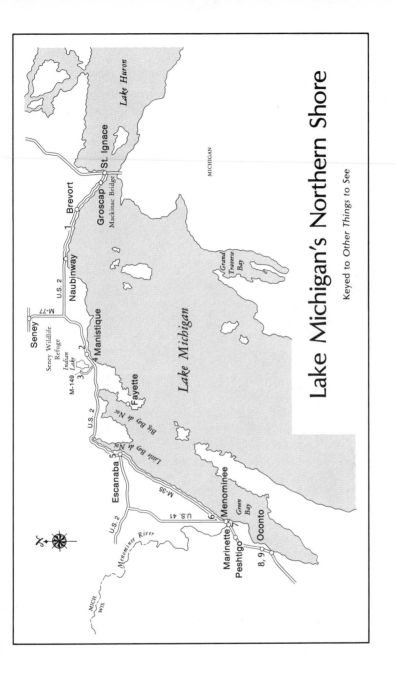

Lake Michigan's Northern Shore

Keyed to *Other Things to See*

than a century, her location and very identity forgotten. Then in 1970 a Wisconsin fisherman caught his nets in a mysterious object on the lake and the *Clark* was rediscovered. A salvage operation managed to bring her to the top intact, and she was floated to Menominee. The *Clark* is berthed on the river, just east of U.S. 41, and is believed to be the oldest freshwater merchant vessel afloat in the country. The ship may be boarded, although she is in need of further restoration below decks. A small museum preserves the artifacts taken from her hold. Known as the Mystery Ship (because her identity was unknown for a year after her discovery), the *Clark* is open daily 8:00 to 8:00, mid-June to mid-September; 9:00 to 6:00 in May, early June, late September, and October. There is an admission charge.

[8]   In about 5500 B.C. a group of people using copper articles and ornaments lived in the area of Oconto, Wisconsin. Their artifacts and burial sites comprise the oldest known collection of cultural materials in the Northeast and some of the earliest examples of metalwork in the world. They lived in a pre-agricultural world, sustaining themselves by hunting, fishing, and collecting wild foods. Their containers were made of bark or skin, rather than pottery. The burial ground is located on county roads west of Oconto. An exhibit case containing several artifacts may be seen in the Beyer Home, a museum of local history at 917 Park Avenue, in the eastern part of town. It is open from Memorial Day to mid-September, daily, 9:00 to 5:00. There is an admission charge, but it will sometimes be waived if you only want to see the Copper Culture display.

[9]   Also located in Oconto is the world's first church structure of the Christian Science faith. The wooden building erected in 1886 is on the corner of Main Street and Chicago Street, just east of U.S. 41. It is open on Wednesday, 7:30 to 8:00 P.M. and Friday, 2:00 to 4:00. There is no admission charge.

Side Trip

In Norway, forty-three miles west of Escanaba on U.S. 2, is the Iron Mountain Iron Mine, once a working operation but now a museum of the industry in the Upper Peninsula. A train makes a half-mile tour of the underground diggings, and there is a museum of antique miner's equipment as well. The mine is located on U.S. 2, one mile west of Norway. It operates from mid-May to mid-October, daily, 9:00 to 6:00. There is an admission charge.

Norway is also the center of an active skiing area. Vulcan USA is located right outside of town, and its season runs from Thanksgiving through March. There are two chair lifts.

State Parks on the Lake

There are two campgrounds directly on Lake Michigan in the Hiawatha National Forest and Mackinac State Forest. Lake Michigan, 17 miles west of St. Ignace, has 38 campsites and a small beach. Hog Island Point, 7 miles east of Naubinway, has 58 campsites on a small roadside tract. There are 69 more camping spots on Brevoort Lake in the national forest, 18 miles west of St. Ignace on U.S. 2 and forest roads. The state forest also has 24 campsites in the Brevoort Lake district, as well as 23 on Big Knob Point, southwest of Naubinway on an unpaved county road.

Indian Lake State Park, 7 miles west of Manistique on Michigan Highway 149, is a 567-acre facility on the lake that is fed by Kitch-iti-ki-pi, the Big Spring. (See Other Things to See for a description of the spring and Palms Book State Park.) The park has an eastern and western unit with beaches, boating facilities, good fishing for bass and walleye, and a museum. There are 305 campsites.

Fayette State Park, 32 miles southwest of Manistique on U.S. 2 and county roads, is described at the beginning of this chapter. There are 80 campsites.

J. W. Wells State Park, 23 miles northeast of Menominee on Michigan Highway 35, has a 2-mile-long beach on Green Bay and one-quarter of a mile of frontage on the Big Cedar River. There are complete recreational facilities in the 974-acre park, with hunting and fishing in designated areas. There are 162 campsites.

The Milwaukee County War Memorial Art Center is the hub of the city's cultural life. *Courtesy the* Detroit News.

7

From Death's Door to Milwaukee

When Jean Nicolet landed near what is now Green Bay, Wisconsin, in 1634, he was convinced that he had found the fabled passage to China. He dressed himself accordingly in damask robes and went ashore firing a pair of muskets to greet any Oriental potentates in the neighborhood. The local Indians took one look at this apparition and fled.

This understandably set back the settlement of Wisconsin's Lake Michigan shore for a while. French missionaries followed Nicolet, trying to locate a remnant of the Huron Nation who had been eradicated in their Georgian Bay homeland by the Iroquois. The Jesuits arrived in 1665 and found a few hundred of their former Indian allies living near the present site of Ashland. The mission begun there was moved to the Green Bay area in 1669; this outpost, under the direction of Fr. Claude Allouez, is regarded as the first permanent settlement in the state. For the next century it was the only one as well.

The voyageurs tracked all across the area, making their discoveries in the Mississippi Valley and Northwest via the waterways of Wisconsin. But no permanent settlements were established because the hostile Fox, the dominant tribe that controlled access to the west, kept the area in turmoil. The Fox

151

opposed France's alliance with the Sioux, and raided trading parties from Quebec. The French managed to lure a sizable segment of the Fox to Detroit in 1712 and had them annihilated by other tribes. This enraged the Fox remaining at home and touched off years of warfare in Wisconsin. Fort La Baye was established in Green Bay in 1717 and became a permanent French base, but the Fox carried on the war even to its gates. Eventually, superior French firepower prevailed; the Fox were removed to the extreme southwestern corner of what would become Wisconsin. They were still there when New France was destroyed in the French and Indian War.

The British, new overlords of the area, didn't stay long. They abandoned the fort at Green Bay during Pontiac's Rebellion in 1763, leaving behind a small French-Canadian settlement. The same kind of outpost also existed at the site of Milwaukee. With the start of the American Revolution, the British sent the H.M.S. *Felicity* on a cruise along Lake Michigan's western shore, trying to whip up enthusiasm for the Loyalist cause among the residents of that area. The local French and Indians were uninterested in the whole affair, or were slightly pro-colonial, and the *Felicity* sailed away. The territory passed into American control after that war, but it was a transition in name only. Nothing really changed. The War of 1812 came and went without making much of a ripple on the lakefront, although there was some action at Prairie du Chien on the Mississippi. This war did indicate to the Americans, however, that it was time to secure these distant lands on the western shore of Lake Michigan. An expedition was sent to Green Bay in 1816. It established Fort Howard with a 300-man garrison, renamed the large island in the bay Washington Island, and raised the Stars and Stripes on the lakefront for good.

The area grew slowly, however, and for a time seemed destined to be carved up at leisure by its neighbors. Illinois helped itself to about 8,000 square miles in 1818 by insisting that it must have the port of Chicago in its boundaries or else become a southern-dominated state. To settle a boundary dispute between Michigan and Ohio over the Toledo area, the federal government gave what is now the Upper Peninsula to Michigan at the expense of Wisconsin. With a population of just 11,000 in 1836 and only recently organized as a territory, Wisconsin could do little more than grumble.

In fourteen years, though, Wisconsin's population had increased almost thirtyfold to over 300,000. The Erie Canal was moving a steady stream of easterners to the new lands of the Northwest. In Europe something just as significant, a lost revolution, was taking place. The abortive revolt in Prussia in 1848 had been crushed and touched off a flood of immigration to America. Wisconsin already had a sizable number of recent arrivals from Germany. The newcomers, seeking ties of language and family, followed them there. Historians have shown that statistically the number of Germans who came to the state as a direct result of the revolution was quite small. Nevertheless, these immigrants exerted a tremendous emotional and intellectual influence; they made Wisconsin into the symbol of a new German homeland for those who followed. By the 1850s, two-thirds of Milwaukee's residents were foreign-born, and of that number two-thirds spoke German as their primary language. There was even some talk of making Wisconsin a German state. Already some smaller communities, like Watertown, were virtually closed to those who spoke only English. But economic control remained firmly in the hands of the earlier immigrants from New England, and nothing came of these Teutonic daydreams. The '48ers did succeed in making Milwaukee one of the country's leading cultural centers during the second half of the nineteenth century, and brought with them a liberal tradition that still permeates the state.

If Jean Nicolet made his Wisconsin landfall today, he'd be hard pressed to determine just where he was. Milwaukee, although retaining strong elements of its Germanic past, is now an ethnic patchwork with dozens of groups making up its content. Racine has one of the largest concentrations of Danes in the country, and Washington Island is noted for its Icelandic settlers. The largest rural Belgian settlement in America is around the village of Brussels in Door County. The Norwegian influence is also strong along the lake. The story goes that Wisconsin promoters would meet new arrivals from Norway in New York with two shills in tow. One of them would be a stooped, emaciated fellow. The promoter said that was what came of living in Illinois. The other was hearty and robust and, said the promoter, a happy resident of Wisconsin. The Norwegians, being no fools, headed for Wisconsin, too. More to the point, the many nautical jobs available in the area coincided with their own economic backgrounds.

Even other states sponsored immigrations to Wisconsin. Charles Turner was sent out by the New York Western Emigration Company in 1835 to locate a likely place for settlement. He got off the boat, obtained a horse, and set off on his search. He got to the Pike River and was thrown by the horse. After spending a night in the open, he decided that place would do as well as any. And that, it is said, was the founding of Kenosha.

The human fabric of Wisconsin's Lake Michigan shore is so varied, in fact, that a modern Nicolet might think he were just about anywhere except China.

A Walk in Milwaukee

Whenever you come across the word *Gemütlichkeit* in an English-language publication, the chances are overwhelmingly good that you are about to read a description of Milwaukee. The city and the word are wedded to each other by culture, history, and temperament—one helping to define the other. This one untranslatable German word stands for the city's heritage, its ambience, and its best-known product. It raises images of jolly blonds in dirndls and lederhosen chugging down Pabst, Schlitz, Blatz, and Miller through endless sunny afternoons punctuated by the blat of a tuba. It conjures up a well-run city populated by law-abiding, God-fearing burghers. Or, as one Milwaukee observer wrote, the word best describes the feeling someone gets "when the food is piled high on the plate, the beer is flowing, and someone from out of town is there to pick up the check."

It's such a nice image and a useful word that one hates to discard it. However, Milwaukee's biggest industry nowadays is electronics equipment; its ethnic slant is as much Polish as German; and, although it has retained a reputation for efficient government, it shares the same problems besetting the country's other older urban areas. Yet something else remains. It is not a particularly beautiful city nor an especially exciting city. But even on a short visit you take away the idea that Milwaukee, above all, is a pleasant city, one that its residents enjoy and take comfort in. As you walk throughout the city, you'll see the places that make Milwaukee so *gemütlich*—including the vestiges of Milwaukee's Teutonic heritage as well as structures as recent as the 1970s.

A walk through Milwaukee might begin in the civic center plaza, on the north side of Wells Street between Seventh and Ninth. This vast open area is surrounded by public buildings. The county courthouse closes off the western end, while the northern side is sealed by the Safety Building on the west and the Police Administration Building to the east. The sprawling complex that houses the Milwaukee Exposition Convention Center and Arena (MECCA to everyone in town) rises on the east, and south of that is the State Office Building. This impressive grouping was envisioned by the pioneer settlers, formally approved in 1919, but not finally rounded out until the 1970s. The two-block-wide plaza is named for Gen. Douglas MacArthur, who grew up and went to school in the city. His only return visit, in 1951, drew the biggest crowds in Milwaukee's history—aside from the World Series celebration of 1957. The plaza is pleasantly landscaped with gardens and shrubs, and on warm afternoons is a favorite lunching spot for workers in the surrounding offices. Centerpiece of the area is a 183-bell carillon set in the front of the Courthouse, atop a clock depicting scenes of Milwaukee in the Gay Nineties.

For more of this ambience, head toward the building on the south end of the plaza, at the head of Eighth Street and Wells. This is the Milwaukee Public Museum, one of the country's best natural history facilities. "The Streets of Old Milwaukee," most popular display in the museum, is a recreation of a downtown street, faithful to the spirit of the late 1800s. Museum officials have tried to gather many authentic artifacts from city businesses of the time, including a room from Milwaukee's most famous house of assignation. The natural history and anthropological sections of the museum are equally absorbing. Displays are freed from the formalized separate-gallery presentation and flow into each other instead, giving a visitor the feeling of being led naturally from one exhibit to the next. The dioramas are especially fine. The furious frozen action of the buffalo hunt is a gripping display, as are the scenes of African wildlife in natural settings. The museum is open daily, 9:00 to 5:00. There is an admission charge for out-of-town visitors.

After leaving the museum head east on Wells to Sixth Street and MECCA. This complex is the home of the Milwaukee Bucks of the National Basketball Association. Numerous conventions, trade shows, and special events are held there, most notably the Holiday Folk Fair, an ethnic extravaganza that goes on the weekend before Thanksgiving. Walk north on Sixth to get some idea of the size of MECCA and turn right when you reach State Street. At Fourth Street, turn left again. Just ahead is a survivor of Milwaukee's Germanic Golden Age, Turner Hall, at 1034 North Fourth. During the second half of the nineteenth century, the city

1 Civic Center Plaza
2 MECCA
3 Milwaukee Public Museum
4 Turner Hall
5 Pere Marquette Park
6 Performing Arts Center
7 Plankinton Building Arcade
8 Iron Block
9 City Hall
10 Pabst Theater
11 Pfister Hotel
12 Federal Building
13 First Wisconsin Center
14 Milwaukee County War Memorial Center

A Milwaukee Walk

was dotted with turnvereins, German gymnastic academies that turned out sound minds as well as bodies with a full range of cultural programs. The institutions had been banned as subversive in Germany, but they flourished here among the liberal '48er political refugees. This brick structure, built in 1882, was the local headquarters. Its interior has been preserved as it looked at that time, with its restaurant one of its chief attractions.

Continue to Highland Street and turn right, then right again at Third Street. In this area there has been an attempt to recapture the flavor of the Germanic era, and a group of restored ethnic shops and restaurants line the street as far as State. Past the corner is Pere Marquette Park, a green space along the Milwaukee River. Just across the water is evidence of the city's contemporary cultural life, the Performing Arts Center. The complex houses symphony, theater, and ballet performances all year round in an award-winning structure. This vantage point gives you a good view of it. You can take a quick walk across the bridge to see what's on during your stay.

Continue south along Plankinton Avenue, which branches off from Third along the river. You are now coming to the central business district, location of most of Milwaukee's retail stores. For a look at one of the city's vintage shopping areas, turn left at Wisconsin Avenue to the Plankinton Building Arcade. Skylighted malls like this one, at 161 West Wisconsin, were the rage in the early years of this century. They are distant ancestors of today's enclosed shopping plazas. The Arcade was built in 1916 and contains shops on three levels around the sunlit central court. A statue of John Plankinton, who financed the structure with a meat-packing fortune, shares the central place of honor with a goldfish pond.

Now return along Wisconsin to the river. You may notice that the bridge jogs sharply as it crosses the water. Almost every bridge across the Milwaukee in the downtown area makes this odd bend. It is one of the last reminders that there were once two separate cities here and they didn't like each other at all. The area you have been walking through once was Kilbourntown. It was named for a promoter who arrived in the area in 1834 and staked out a city on the west bank of the river. His activity was greeted with curiosity by the residents of Juneautown on the river's eastern side. Juneautown dated from 1817 (more or less) when Solomon Juneau, a strapping French Canadian, arrived from Green Bay to set up a fur trade station. By 1831 the collection of cabins around the outpost was incorporated into a city. But Byron Kilbourn decided to ignore its presence. His street plan was purposely lined up out of kilter with that of the rival town, and he refused to acknowledge its very existence. When it came time to build a bridge, Kilbourn turned south to the Menomonee River and linked his settlement to yet a third town in the vicinity, started by George Walker. Juneautown still had the largest population but saw its future threatened by this sudden isolation from the other communities. The residents of the older town persuaded the territory to authorize a bridge across the Milwaukee to link it with Kilbourntown. A bridge was built; the Kilbourn bunch knocked it down. At one point, residents of the two towns faced off across the river with cannon in an attempt to settle the matter without resorting to amicability. Bloodshed was averted, and the towns were eventually joined to form Milwaukee. Still the argument raged. The west siders from Kilbourntown adamantly opposed the bridge; the east siders from Juneautown stoutly demanded it. Not until 1846 was the issue finally settled—but the bridges still jog in the middle as a reminder of Milwaukee's disjointed union.

Across the bridge at the corner of Wisconsin and Water Street is the Iron Block, an unusual structure put up after the Civil War. Its cast iron facing was meant to mimic the appearance of fashionable eastern shops of the day, in an attempt at winning over the carriage trade. On the intersection's northwest side is the site of Juneau's cabin, the first house in Milwaukee.

Walk north on Water past some of the city's oldest business addresses. City Hall, a spectacular building modeled loosely on the great governmental palaces of the Flemish Renaissance, dominates the view before you. Its 393-foot spire was completed in 1895, in the midst of a boom that shaped the downtown area. It cost one million dollars, a princely sum in those years, and the soaring sandstone tower has given the city its money's worth over the decades. The bell within the tower bears the inscription:

"When I sound the hour of day, / From this grand and lofty steeple, / Deem it a reminder, pray, / To be honest with the people." The bell is no longer rung. For information on tours of City Hall, call 278-3285.

Across Water on the west is the Pabst Theater, the cultural center of its era, opened the same year as its neighbor. It was famous for its German-language productions and helped win Milwaukee its nineteenth-century nickname "Athens of the Midwest." The theater has just come through an ambitious restoration and houses theatrical productions on a regular basis. You may be able to join a tour group during weekdays by calling 271-4747.

Head east on Wells three blocks to Jefferson Street and turn right. This is an interesting area of shops and art galleries housed in restored homes and office buildings. At the corner of Mason Street is another of the city's nineteenth-century landmarks, the Pfister Hotel. Its opening in 1893 was a gala event, and it has remained at the center of the city's history ever since. The Pfister is still regarded as Milwaukee's finest. Take a look at the elegantly restored lobby to see why.

Leave the hotel by the Wisconsin Avenue exit and turn left, past more structures from the 1890s. On the next block is the Federal Building, a somber and imposing mass, while two blocks further is the Greek Revival temple of the Northwestern Mutual Life Insurance Building. Different styles, same era. Just beyond is the city's only skyscraper, the forty-two-story First Wisconsin Center.

Turn left on Marshall Street, which still retains vestiges of an earlier life as Milwaukee's Gold Coast, a street of mansions and townhouses. Then go right on Mason. Directly in front of you, across a pedestrian overpass, is the splendid Milwaukee County War Memorial Art Center. One of the last commissions of architect Eero Saarinen, the building occupies a spectacular site on the lakefront, commanding views along the entire breadth of the city's shoreline. Completed in 1957, the memorial honors city residents killed in World War II, Korea, and Vietnam. Inside is the Art Center, housing a good collection of Old Masters and, as might be expected, nineteenth-century German art. In addition to the paintings, there is a group of Meissen porcelains and antique beer mugs. A new wing houses the twentieth-century art collection donated by Mrs. Harry Lynde Bradley. There is also an outstanding assortment of examples of decorative art and furniture. The center is open from 10:00 to 5:00, except on Monday. There is an admission charge.

Walk onto the lake gallery of the building. To the north are the beaches, parks, and marinas that make the Milwaukee lakefront one of the loveliest in the country. To the south is the entrance to the harbor, among the busiest on the Lakes. Two annual festivals are held on adjacent property. To the north is the Lakefront Festival, an outdoor art fair supported by the Art Center. It is held in June. To the south of the Center is the more ambitious Summerfest, a ten-day program of concerts, name entertainment, sporting events, and exhibitions. It usually runs in early July.

The Brewers

Was it really a beer that made Milwaukee famous? Not according to the statistics. There has been only one year—1889—in which brewing was the city's leading industry by dollar volume. But what does fame have to do with statistics? For almost one hundred years the link between beer and Milwaukee has been formed in the American mind by advertising and promotions. "The beer that made Milwaukee famous"; "I'm from Milwaukee and I ought to know"; "Whenever they mention the town of Milwaukee you think of beer." The two are inseparable. Visiting the city without taking a brewery tour would be like going to New Orleans and passing up the Dixieland: simply unthinkable.

There have been breweries in Milwaukee since the 1840s, but they were small-scale affairs at first. Owned by English immigrants, they turned out a top-fermentation beer that didn't keep long and could not be exported. In the next twenty years, however, several developments combined to throw beer and Milwaukee together:

- German immigration to the city rapidly increased the demand for the drink.
- Pioneer wheat farmers in Wisconsin began raising hops to supplement their crops, thus giving brewers a dependable source of supply. There was also an abundance of natural ice in the area and cheap cooperage for the barrels in which all beer was packaged.
- The lager process was perfected in Germany and transported to Milwaukee. This bottom-fermentation method enabled the beer to last longer and to travel.
- Taxes on alcoholic beverages were raised during the Civil War—one dollar a gallon on whisky and one dollar a barrel on beer. That formula substantially boosted the price of a shot of whisky, and workingmen began switching to the less expensive drink. Beer won itself an expanded market.

Meanwhile, the great breweries that would survive into the next century were being formed. Herman Reuthlisberger was the first German immigrant to enter the brewing business. His Melms beer was the city's favorite through the 1850s, but it had many rivals. In 1844 Jacob Best switched from the vinegar game to brewing, and his beer was an immediate success. The business eventually went into the hands of his nephews and nieces. In 1864 one of the nieces married a young Great Lakes ship's captain, Frederick Pabst. By the next year Pabst was running the brewery, and Best was on its way to becoming the nineteenth century's largest-selling beer. In 1889 a grateful board of directors voted to change the name of the product to Pabst. "Blue Ribbon" was added to the title in the 1890s after the beer won several awards in national competitions. For a time, the ribbons were actually attached by hand to the bottles, which must have made a cheerful sight.

Two years after Best's enterprise began, John Braun started brewing a beer. His foreman was a brewer's son from Mittenberg-on-the-Main, Valentin Blatz. When Braun died, Blatz married his widow, and another Milwaukee firm had its name. One of the Best nephews started a brewery on Plank Road, and named the beer after the address. He sold out in 1855 to Frederick Miller, and a third brewing giant was in business.

August Krug joined the brewers in 1849. He, too, left a widow who remarried one of the company employees, bookkeeper Joseph Schlitz. He ran the company until he was lost at sea on what was to have been a triumphal return home to Germany. Schlitz had observed what happened to the other breweries when the founder passed on, and before leaving on his trip he had redrawn his will stipulating that the company name never be changed. Although the brewery has been run by the Uihlein family for the last one hundred years, their name has never appeared on the label. (It does appear, however, on one of the auditoriums in Milwaukee's Performing Arts Center. The family has been a noted city benefactor.)

In 1852, the Milwaukee brewers made their first tentative move towards the out-of-town market, exporting 645 barrels. In seventeen years the figure was up to 50,000 barrels, over half of their total production. Opportunistic brewery representatives poured into Chicago after the great fire had destroyed that city's beer-making plants. The new customers boosted Milwaukee sales by 44 percent and gave it a permanent lock on the Chicago market.

In the next three decades production multiplied twenty-six times. Although other American cities had fine breweries, Milwaukee alone turned out beers for a national market. Situated in a smaller city, the breweries aggressively sought out customers everywhere. By the turn of the century, Milwaukee was producing three times the beer per capita as New York, five times as much as Chicago.

Blatz came up with the idea of selling beer in bottles in 1875. That made product identification essential, and the major brewers began a battle of advertising and promotion, each of them emphasizing their ties with the city. Schlitz was the most succesful with its "beer that made Milwaukee famous" line, a national catch-phrase by 1890. Schlitz made Pabst drop a similar slogan and sued New York brewers who tried to use the name "Milwaukee beer" on their products. Schlitz and Pabst sponsored beer gardens and dance halls around the city and even built hotels in other American towns. Pabst would hire actors to walk into taverns, buy a round of his product for the house, and drink to the Captain's health.

Many of the smaller breweries went under during Prohibition. The big ones survived by producing things like candy and machinery, and then came back bigger than ever after the Eighteenth Amendment's repeal. The industry began to decentralize in the 1930s, setting up satellite breweries in many areas of the country to get the beer to the customer faster. Miller, buoyed by the success of its low-calorie Lite beer, became the top-seller in Milwaukee into the 1970s. Through it all, the city remains at the symbolic center of the industry.

Three breweries offer tours through their Milwaukee plants—Miller, Pabst, and Schlitz. The tours offer roughly similar run-throughs of the brewing operations and culminate in tasting of the product in a hospitality room.

The Pabst Brewing Company, at 901 West Juneau Avenue, offers tours on the hour from 9:00 to 11:00 and 1:00 to 4:00, Monday through Friday; Saturday, 9:00 to 11:00. Tours of the

Joseph Schlitz Brewing Company, at 234 West Galena Street, are given from 9:00 to 3:30, Monday through Friday. The Miller Brewing Company, at 4000 West State Street, gives its tours from 9:00 to 4:00, Monday through Friday; on Saturday from May to November, from 8:00 to 2:00. There is no charge for any of the brewery tours.

Door Peninsula

To the French it was Death's Door, Porte des Morts, a narrow treacherous strait that snared ships upon its deadly rocks. The name was later extended to the adjacent mainland peninsula, although the first part of the ominous nickname was omitted. To the holiday crowds that turn the peninsula into Chicago's most northerly suburb each summer, it is simply Door County, "Cape Cod of the Midwest."

If Door County resembles any part of New England it would more likely be Maine than the gentle beaches of the Massachusetts cape. The Door's stern cliffs and rocky shore recall a rougher and less amiable coast than Cape Cod's, yet its scenery and faint air of nostalgia do have the texture of a wayward slice of New England. Comparison to Cape Cod will do as well as to anywhere else.

Sturgeon Bay is the county seat, leading commercial center, and focus of the Door. South of here the county is primarily agricultural, dominated by the Belgian settlements around Brussels, Wisconsin. To the north, it is solid resort territory. The dividing line is the Sturgeon Bay Canal, blasted through the limestone of this narrow neck of land in 1878. The place had been a portaging point for two centuries. Travelers saved themselves a 100-mile voyage around the top of the Door, a journey as perilous as it was long, by crossing here from Lake Michigan to Green Bay. The canal made Sturgeon Bay an important northern port.

Although it is not the oldest town in the county (that distinction belongs to Baileys Harbor on the lake side), Sturgeon Bay's location has always been important. It was visited by Fr. Jacques Marquette in 1673, and it was here, seven years later, that Henry Tonty and three other starving survivors of an Indian uprising in Illinois came for rescue. The men had made their way from the area of Peoria through the dark Wisconsin forests in an attempt to contact their leader, Robert LaSalle. They were reduced to chewing their own moccasins for food before they were rescued by a band of Potawatomi. LaSalle County Park, southeast of town, marks the site of this meal. You can picnic there now, perhaps on a more appetizing diet. Potawatomi State Park is located northwest of town. It is a 1,126-acre shoreline facility offering a full

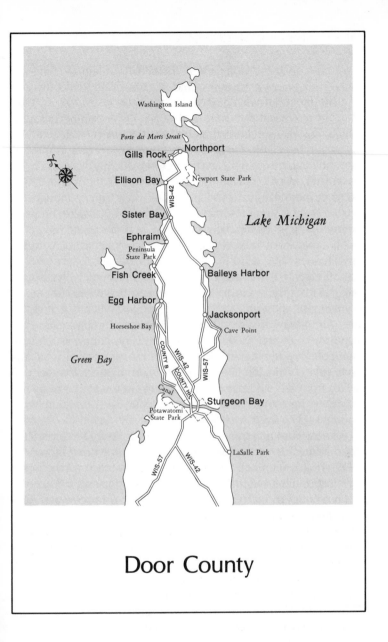

Door County

assortment of water sports. Door, incidentally, claims to have the longest lakeshore (250 miles) and the most state parks (five) of any county in the United States.

The town got its name from the pioneer fishing industry, which took thousands of sturgeon from the nearby waters. It was also a lumber camp. Now its main source of income is the surrounding cherry orchards. Martin Orchard, north of town on County Road HH, claims to be the largest in the world. Many orchards permit travelers to pick their own fruit. Although the orchard land is slowly being reduced (about 4,000 acres produce ten million pounds annually in the county), blossomtime, in the last two weeks of May, remains one of the loveliest parts of the year here.

Sturgeon Bay has a county historical museum, with displays ranging from the time of the Winnebago Indians to the age of tourism. The museum, at Fourth Avenue and Michigan Street, is open mid-May to mid-October, Tuesday through Saturday, 10:00 to noon and 1:00 to 5:00. There is no admission charge. Sturgeon Bay is also the departure point for boat trips up the peninsula aboard the *Good Ship Lollipop*, a 31-foot vessel that leaves from the old state highway bridge in town. The tours run from late June through Labor Day. Hours and duration vary. Call 743-4377 for current information.

If you want to explore the Door by car, leave town on State Road 42 for the north. There is also a shoreline drive by way of county roads B and G, but private cottages screen off the water for most of the route. If you take the latter, Horseshoe Bay Park, just south of Egg Harbor, does provide access to the water, and the drive is a good deal more leisurely than on the busy state road.

There are two explanations of the origin of Egg Harbor's name. The first is that a pioneer settler, Increase Claflin, came across many duck eggs on the shore. The second story is much better. A group of well-to-do Green Bay residents, on a summertime excursion in 1825, sailed into the harbor for a picnic. In an excess of high spirits, the picnickers pulled out dozens of eggs intended for their meal and threw them between the boats instead. The battle continued on land and left the shoreline littered with shells as far as the eye could see. The merry crowd from

Green Bay then decided the place should henceforth be called Egg Harbor. If this story is not true, it definitely should be. The village perches atop a bluff, and there is a fine view from its marina at the foot of the hill. There is also a museum in town dedicated to Oshkosh, last chief of the Menominee. It contains many of his possessions, as well as artifacts of other area Indians. It is open from mid-June to Labor Day, daily, 9:00 to 6:00. There is an admission charge.

The next town along State Road 42 is Fish Creek, which offers the most interesting shopping in the area. Founder's Square, in the center of town, is an inviting collection of crafts shops, art studios, and boutiques housed in a variety of nineteenth-century structures. Right across the street is Proud Mary, a stylish Victorian hotel and shopping plaza. It was built across the bay in Marinette in 1889 and moved here over the ice about fifteen years later.

Fish Creek sits in an indentation in the bayside bluffs and was settled by the same Claflin who came upon all the duck eggs in the neighboring village. But not until Asa Thorp built a pier here in 1853, the only one north of Green Bay on the peninsula, did the place prosper. (Thorp's home is now part of Founder's Square.) Fish Creek remains the entertainment capital of the area. The Peninsula Players is the oldest summer stock company in the country, putting on theatrical productions here since 1935. The Playhouse is located on the bay three miles south of town in an all-weather pavilion surrounded by gardens. Productions run from the last week of June to Labor Day, nightly except Monday. The Peninsula Music Festival is held annually for two weeks in August in the town's Gibraltar Auditorium. The programs feature visiting artists in symphonic concerts.

Yet a third theatrical company performs in nearby Peninsula State Park, between Fish Creek and Ephraim. The Heritage Ensemble puts on dramas drawn from regional history and folklore. The productions in the State Park Amphitheater are held every night but Sunday from July 1 to Labor Day. The park itself is a sprawling, 3,767-acre recreation ground, occupying a scenic headland extending into the bay. There are nine miles of beaches, a golf course, bridle paths, water sports facilities, and scenic overlooks that open out on clear days all the way to the Lake Michigan shoreline across the bay. Also in the park is the Eagle Bluff Lighthouse, dating from 1868 and restored to its appearance of a century ago. The lighthouse is open from mid-June to Labor Day, 10:00 to 6:00. There is an admission charge.

The most appealing view in Door County is north across the inlet to the town of Ephraim with its wooden homes and churches climbing from the water to the bluffs behind. Here, if ever, the Door resembles New England. The photogenic village has an equally picturesque past. Ephraim means "very fruitful" in Hebrew. The name was given to the town by its Norwegian inhabitants who settled there in 1853 after their earlier Moravian religious colony in Green Bay was torn apart by dissension. The Green Bay colony was formed when a wealthy Norwegian immigrant, Nils Otto Tank, purchased land in that city and invited a group of Moravian co-religionists from Milwaukee to settle on it. All property was to be held in common, in accord with church teachings. The colonists, however, were mostly refugees from the near feudal economy of Norway and were suspicious of their wealthy patron. They suspected him of trying to impose a new sort of religious feudalism on them. When he refused to give individuals title to the land, the colony split apart. One group, led by theological student A. M. Iverson, came to Door County. Their landing here is commemorated by the Moravian Monument in the harbor. Other historic buildings preserve relics of the first settlers. The Pioneer Schoolhouse, on the bluff at Moravia Street and County Road Q, dates from 1869 and has displays of local history and art exhibits. It is open from July to Labor Day, 9:00 to 5:00, except Sunday. There is no admission charge. Nearby is the Old Moravian Church. Anderson Store, north of town on Highway 42, is a restored pioneer general store with more Moravian memorabilia. It is open daily, except Sunday, from mid-June to Labor Day, 10:00 to noon and 2:00 to 5:00. After Labor Day, it is open weekends until the second week in October.

Ephraim puts on a Fyr-Ball, or Scandinavian welcome to summer, on the third weekend of June each year. Highlights of the celebration are the coronation of a Viking chieftain and a community fish boil. You'll see ads for fish boils all around the county. They are something like Wisconsin's answer to the Hawaiian luau. In their most refined form they are held right on the beach with all sorts of elaborate ceremonies. Almost every restaurant in the county holds a fish boil on specified nights during the summer. The boil actually consists of a huge fish stew, with trout or whitefish as the principal ingredient. This is mixed with potatoes and onions and served with melted butter. There are those gourmands who would drive an entire weekend to attend one. Fish boils are, at the very least, a distinct part of the local color.

North of Ephraim, the coast gets rougher and the towns less interesting. Sister Bay is a more contemporary-looking place than its neighbors and is a shopping center for the northern half of the peninsula. Because the two state highways, 42 and 57, converge here, it is also the most congested part of the county. It is noted for its offshore islands, breeding grounds for gulls and terns.

Ellison Bay, the next stop north, is a tiny village; beyond it is Gills Rock, landing place of the ferry to Washington Island (see Other Things to See). Gills Rock is a picturesque sort of place. Unfortunately, ferryboat traffic can back up so densely during the summer that it is almost impossible to find a parking place in town. The road continues on to Northport, at the very top of the peninsula. Northport has a good blufftop viewpoint over the treacherous strait that gave its name to the entire county. Return-ing, just south of Gills Rock is the road to Newport State Park, a less developed area on Lake Michigan with 2,017 acres of beach, forest, and backpacking trails.

Back in Sister Bay, Highway 57 branches to the southeast to the lake side of the peninsula. This is a far less crowded section of the county, and after the crush of the bay side towns it can come as a relief. The leading center is Baileys Harbor, which stretches out along a crescent beach. The harbor was discovered in 1848. The town was settled three years later, originally under the name of Gibraltar. Stop at the little park south of town and walk out along the rocky pier for a lovely look at the surrounding scene. Just north of town is the Ridges, a sanctuary for native plants and animals. Only foot travel is permitted in the area, and protective regulations are strictly enforced. There is no admission charge, but visitors are asked to check in at the orientation center. The Ridges is noted for its wildflowers and twenty-five species of orchids. Also in the vicinity are the Range Lights, a pair of beacons built in 1870 to guide ships into Baileys Harbor. They are still in operation.

South from Baileys Harbor is the village of Jacksonport. Beyond that is the turnout to Cave Point County Park, where a scenic drive through thick forests leads to an area of lakeside bluffs that have been shaped into arches, ledges, and caves by the pounding of the waves. A thin shelf of rock extends out from the bluffs to the lake. There are legends that one of the caves extends all the way underneath the peninsula and emerges in Green Bay. A lake steamer carrying a cargo of corn was wrecked near here, the stories say, and later the corn was found floating on the bay side. From this point, county roads angle southwest back to Highway 57. That route then runs uninterrupted to Sturgeon Bay and the end of the circuit of the Door.

Other Things to See

[1]   Green Bay is immediately identifiable all across the continent because of its professional football team, the Packers. But the city at the mouth of the Fox River also happens to be the oldest settlement in Wisconsin, with a rich past in other areas besides the gridiron. Hazelwood, a fine colonnaded mansion dating from 1837, was owned by Morgan L. Martin, president of the convention that drew up Wisconsin's Constitution. The drafting of much of that document was done in Hazelwood. It is located on the east bank of the Fox at 1008 South Monroe Avenue. Hazelwood is open Tuesday through Saturday, 10:00 to 5:00, April to October and on Sunday 2:00 to 5:00; rest of the year, Tuesday through Saturday, 1:00 to 5:00. There is an admission charge.

[2]   A few miles further south along the river the state has gathered fourteen buildings that either illustrate or figure prominently in the history of Wisconsin. Heritage Hill State Park is on a slope above the river's eastern bank, on Wisconsin 57 between Green Bay and DePere. Among the star attractions are: the Tank Cottage, built in 1776 and believed to be the oldest surviving house in the state (it was later occupied by Nils Tank, whose wealth supported the Moravian colony that moved to Ephraim in Door County [see Door Peninsula Section, this chapter]); buildings from the Fort Howard stockade, erected to guard Green Bay in 1816; and the Cotton House, an 1840 Greek Revival gem that has been furnished in the style of the period. Heritage Hill is open daily, May through Labor Day, 9:00 to 5:00. There is an admission charge.

[3]   Green Bay is one of the most important rail centers of the north and, appropriately enough, it is the site of the National Railroad Museum. This sprawling complex on the west bank of the Fox, at 2285 South Broadway, was intended as a tribute to the Age of Steam. There are several vintage locomotives and cars and a restored small town depot on the grounds. The exhibits also crowd over into more recent times, with some of the last luxury passenger trains, as well as staff cars associated with Dwight Eisenhower and Winston Churchill, on display. Be sure

From Death's Door
to Milwaukee

Keyed to *Other Things to See*

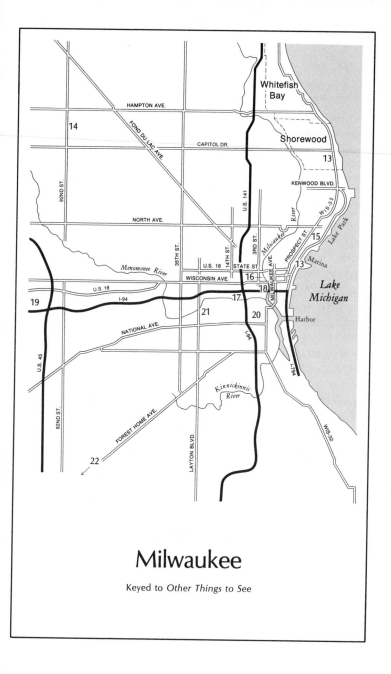

Milwaukee

Keyed to *Other Things to See*

to take in the enormous "Big Boy" locomotive of the Union Pacific, weighing in at 3,810 tons. Rides may be taken on standard-gauge trains that circle the grounds at regular intervals. Uneven labelling keeps this from being an outstanding museum, but it is an interesting stop even for those whose only rail trip has been on a subway. The museum is open daily, Memorial Day to Labor Day, 9:00 to 5:00. It is open only on weekends during the remainder of May and September. There is an admission charge that also covers the rail ride.

[4]   For those who find Green Bay absolutely inseparable from the Packers, a museum devoted to the football team is adjacent to the stadium. It is located at Oneida Street and Lombardi Drive and contains memorabilia of all the Packers from Curley Lambeau to John Brockington. It is open daily, 10:00 to 5:00. There is an admission charge.

[5]   Washington Island is separated from the Wisconsin mainland by the strait known as "Death's Door." The ships wrecked in these waters number well into the hundreds. Old legends tell of a never-ending ghostly gale that churns the waters and of undercurrents so strong they can dissolve two feet of ice in twelve hours. The island contains the oldest Icelandic settlement in the United States, dating to 1870. Other Scandinavian groups with strong traditions also live there. They hold an annual festival on the first weekend in August. A small museum on Little Lake Road in the island's northwest corner contains exhibits on the island's history. It is open from July to Labor Day, 10:00 to 4:30; in late May and June and September to mid-October, from 11:30 to 3:30. There is a small admission charge. There is daily ferry service to Gills Rock, weather permitting. During the summer season boats operate hourly from 7:00 A.M. to 6:30 P.M., more frequently at peak periods. The island is a continuation of the Door Peninsula and has the same striking scenery.

[6]   Rock Island once was owned entirely by Chicago manufacturer C. H. Thordarson, who put up a great hall in the Icelandic feudal style. The building still stands, but the island is now a state park. No vehicles are permitted on the 783-acre island. Access is by passenger ferry from Jackson Harbor on the northeastern corner of Washington Island. There are swimming, boat-

ing, and picnic facilities available and forty tent sites for those who really want a place to get away. On the northern tip of Rock Island is the Potawatomi Lighthouse, dating from 1836.

[7]   The Von Stiehl Winery in Algoma is the oldest in the state, specializing in sweet cherry and other fruit blends from the nearby orchards. There is a tour of the winery offered, with wine and cheese tasting at its conclusion. The winery is situated in a lovely spot at the head of the harbor, at 115 Navarino Street. (Signs point the route from the main highway.) The site is dominated by the impressive steeple of St. Mary's Catholic Church across the harbor. The winery is open daily, 9:00 to 5:00, May through October.

[8]   Also on the Algoma waterfront is Harbor Village, a small commercial development highlighted by the Living Lakes Expo. Series of animated displays and electronic exhibits illustrate aspects of Great Lakes history, with special reference to the fishing industry. Located at 80 Church Street, opposite the winery, it is open daily, 10:00 to 5:00. There is an admission charge.

[9]   The Algoma Railroad offers two-hour excursions into the wooded hill country of Kewaunee County. The train goes to Casco Junction, then turns around after a brief stop. There are trains at 11:00 and 2:00 daily from mid-June to Labor Day, and on weekends from Memorial Day through late October. There is one daily weekend trip at 2:00 P.M. from Labor Day to mid-October. Trains leave from the Algoma Railroad depot on Highway 42.

[10]   Kewaunee, a scenic town surrounded by hills, was the birthplace of the car ferry service across Lake Michigan. It began here in 1892, and the town is still the western terminus of the ferries from Frankfort, Michigan. It is also the home of Swaboda Furniture, specialists in grandfather clocks and wooden church installations. Their showroom is on Highway 42. Fifteen miles south of town, near Two Creeks, is the Point Beach Nuclear Power Plant. An information center on Wisconsin 42 has exhibits and films on this source of energy. It is open daily, April to October, 10:00 to 5:00; rest of the year, weekends only. There is no admission charge.

[11]   Manitowoc's economic life has always been bound to

the lake at its front door. Shipbuilding and fishing were staple industries in its early years, giving the city a nautical flavor matched by few Great Lakes ports. The Maritime Museum and Submariners Memorial tries to preserve some of that color. The museum, on South Eighth Street at the Manitowoc River, is devoted to the history of this part of the Great Lakes, with special reference to the ships built at local yards. Among them were several World War II submarines. The U.S.S. *Cobia,* a veteran of two years in the Pacific campaign, is meant to symbolize that era. It is anchored in a small park across the street from the museum and may be toured. A combination ticket is available for the two attractions, or each may be visited separately. The museum is open daily, 9:00 to 5:00, June to Labor Day; rest of the year, 10:00 to 4:00 on weekdays, 10:00 to 5:00 on weekends. The submarine has similar hours, but is open only on weekends from Labor Day to Memorial Day, 10:00 to 4:00.

[12]   One of the smaller Wisconsin towns that became a center of German immigration was Sheboygan. At one time it was called "Bratwurst Capital of the World," but the major economic force in the city was the plumbing fixture plant of the Kohler family. Walter J. Kohler, who later became governor of Wisconsin, set up the company town of Kohler (four miles west of the city along the Sheboygan River). He also built Waelderhaus, a reconstruction of the Kohler ancestral home in the Austrian Alps. The chalet on West Riverside Drive is open daily, 2:00 to 5:00. There is no admission charge.

[13]   Highway 32 is a pleasant drive through Milwaukee's prosperous northern suburbs. It winds past stately homes along the lake, into the city, and through Milwaukee's outstanding system of waterfront parks. Cut off the highway at Lincoln Memorial Drive, just past Kenwood Boulevard, for the road through the parks. An especially attractive area is the marina at McKinley Park. The system of parks and beaches stretches north for three and a half miles from the War Memorial Center.

[14]   The Annunciation Greek Orthodox Church was the last major work of architect Frank Lloyd Wright. This striking, saucer-shaped structure has a blue dome supported by concrete

walls. It is open daily, except Sunday, 10:00 to 4:00. On Saturdays, a guide must accompany visitors. There is a small admission charge. The church is located at 9000 West Congress Street on Milwaukee's far northwest side.

[15]   The Villa Terrace houses a fine museum of furniture and decorative art encompassing the period 1660 to 1820. The Italianate home, built in 1923, also is an attraction in itself. It is situated on a lakeside bluff, and its gardens and fountains cascade down towards the lakeside. The museum, at 2220 North Terrace Avenue, may be reached from downtown Milwaukee by taking Highway 32 to Kenilworth Street and going right for three blocks to Terrace. The museum is open June through December, Wednesday to Sunday, 1:00 to 5:00; weekends only, January to March; weekends and Wednesday, rest of the year. There is no admission charge.

[16]   The Milwaukee County Historical Society Museum is housed in a building that is a landmark in itself. The old Second Ward Savings Bank was once known as the Brewers Bank and its president was a Blatz. Besides its own fine architecture, the building at 910 North Third Street has exhibits on the city's history, antique vehicles, and memorabilia of Douglas MacArthur's family. It is open Monday to Saturday, 9:00 to 5:00; Sunday, 1:00 to 5:00. There is no admission charge.

[17]   The campus of Marquette University, a Jesuit institution with an enrollment of about 12,000, lies along Wisconsin Avenue, just west of the central business district. Most notable sight on campus is the Joan of Arc Chapel, brought here from the village of Chasse, France, in 1966. The saint is said to have prayed there, and the stone she kissed before her execution is implanted in the wall near the altar. The fifteenth-century chapel was reassembled stone by stone on its present site, at 601 North Fourteenth Street. It is open daily, 10:00 to 4:00. There is no admission charge.

[18]   Tours of Milwaukee's busy harbor are given on the 150-passenger vessel *Iroquois,* which once ran between Mackinac Island and the mainland. The two-hour cruises take in the lakefront and the Milwaukee River as well as the harbor area.

Cruises run at 1:00 and 3:30, Memorial Day to Labor Day, with an additional cruise at 7:00 P.M. after July 1. The dock is at the Clybourn Street bridge and the Milwaukee River.

[19]   The most noted feature of the Milwaukee County Zoo is its natural settings; predators and their prey are grouped as they would be in the wild, but are kept apart by hidden moats. There is also a good nocturnal animal section. A miniature train makes a circuit of the 184-acre site. The zoo is located on U.S. 18 (Blue Mound Road) in the western extremity of the city. It is open from 9:30 to 7:00 in summer, to 4:30 in winter. Hours vary at other seasons. There is an admission charge.

[20]   Walker's Point was the third pioneer settlement that eventually, along with Kilbourntown and Juneautown, became modern Milwaukee. But this area, on the south bank of the Menomonee River, retained a strong sense of identity and is now the city's best-preserved historic neighborhood. The area land-mark is the four-sided clock of the Allen-Bradley Building. The 280-foot high building dominates the skyline south of down-town. Tours are given through the neighborhood from 9:30 to 4:00 on weekdays, leaving from 414 West National Avenue (Wisconsin 15). Call 645-9222 for schedule information.

[21]   Three glass domes in Mitchell Park create artificial climates much different from anything found in Milwaukee. Two of the domes of the Horticultural Conservatory enable plants from arid deserts and humid jungles to flourish along the south bank of the Menomonee River. The third dome is used for special seasonal exhibits. The eighty-five-foot-high domes are sur-rounded by sunken gardens and pools. The domes are open 9:00 to 9:00, Tuesday to Sunday; Monday to 5:00. There is an admis-sion charge.

[22]   The Experimental Aircraft Association Museum con-tains about 100 planes, ranging from antiques to Gemini training craft. It is the largest private collection of aircraft in the country. Star attractions are World War I combat planes, a rep-lica of Charles A. Lindbergh's *Spirit of St. Louis,* and the smallest plane ever built. The museum is located in Franklin, at 11311 West Forest Home Avenue, southwest of Milwaukee on Wiscon-

sin 100. It is open 8:30 to 5:00, Monday to Saturday; 11:00 to 5:00 on Sunday. There is an admission charge.

[23]   The Administration Building of the Johnson Wax Company has been a nationally recognized landmark from the day Frank Lloyd Wright completed it at Racine in 1939. The banded glass tower, which duplicates the shape of a can of its inhabitant's product, may be toured on weekdays from 9:15 to 3:15, June through August; 10:15 to 2:15, rest of the year. Adjoining the building is the Golden Rondelle, a theater that originally was built as the Johnson exhibition at the New York World's Fair of 1964–65. It was relocated here in 1967. Films are screened daily on its triple-image viewing surface. The complex is located on Fourteenth Street, just east of Highway 32, in central Racine. There is no admission charge for either the tour or the film.

[24]   A lovely series of waterfront parks that run almost the entire length of the city have kept Kenosha's lakefront uncluttered. Kenosha, however, is a busy industrial city, and the manufacturing center of the country's fourth largest automobile maker, American Motors Corporation. Tours of the assembly line, at 5626 Twenty-fifth Avenue, are given at 9:15 and 1:15 on weekdays, but are sometimes suspended in midsummer.

Side Trips

The Fox Cities of Appleton and Neenah-Menasha, forty miles southwest of Green Bay on U.S. 41, make up the center of Wisconsin's giant paper industry. The Institute of Paper Chemistry is in Appleton. Its Dard Hunter Museum, illustrating the history of papermaking from its inception, is located at 1043 East South River Road and is open Monday through Friday, 8:30 to 4:30. There is no admission charge. In Neenah-Menasha is the Bergstrom Art Center with its collection of one thousand glass paperweights, along with antique German glass and other changing exhibits. Located at 165 North Park Avenue, Neenah, it is open Tuesday through Thursday and weekends, June to August, 1:00 to 5:00. The rest of the year, the days are Wednesday, Thursday, and weekends. There is no admission charge.

In Greenbush, nineteen miles west of Sheboygan on State Highway 23, is the Old Wade House, a stagecoach inn built in 1845 on the new road to Fond du Lac. Now a state park, the complex also includes other cabins, a blacksmith shop, and a carriage museum reached by horse-drawn cart. The park is open daily, May to October, 9:00 to 5:00. There is an admission charge.

In Campbellsport, thirty-six miles southwest of Sheboygan on State Highway 67, are the headquarters of Kettle Moraine State Forest. The moraine is a deposit left by the retreat of the glaciers in the most recent Ice Age, the one that shaped the Great Lakes. There are scenic drives, geological exhibits, and recreational facilities throughout the forest.

In Watertown, forty-two miles northwest of Milwaukee on U.S. 16, is the first kindergarten in America, established by Mrs. Carl Schurz in 1856 when this was an almost completely German community. It is on the grounds of Octagon House, a fifty-seven-room mansion with many unusual features. The house and classroom are open daily, May to October, 10:00 to 5:00. There is an admission charge.

State Parks on the Lake

Potawatomi, 2 miles northwest of Sturgeon Bay on County Road C, is described in the Door Peninsula section of this chapter. There are 123 campsites in the 1,126-acre facility.

Peninsula, 2 miles northeast of Fish Creek on State Highway 42, is also described with the Door Peninsula. There are 520 campsites in the huge, 3,763-acre park.

Newport, 4 miles south of Gills Rock on State Highway 42, is described with the Door Peninsula as well. There are 12 primitive tent spaces in the 2,017-acre park.

Rock Island, accessible by ferryboat from Washington Island, is described in Other Things to See. There are 40 tent spaces on the 783-acre island.

Point Beach State Forest, 14 miles north of Manitowoc on State Highways 42 and 177, has full recreational facilities and a beach on the Lake Michigan dunes. There are 152 campsites.

Terry Andrae–John M. Kohler, 4 miles south of Sheboygan

on U.S. 141, is a 750-acre facility with water recreation, picnicking, riding, and a nature center. There are 105 campsites.

Harrington Beach, 25 miles south of Sheboygan on U.S. 141, is a day-use facility with an excellent Lake Michigan beach. There are no campsites.

Public beaches are plentiful along the lakeshore in Milwaukee and Kenosha. Bradford Beach, along Lincoln Memorial Drive north of downtown, is the best in Milwaukee. There is no camping.

The masts of pleasure craft are dwarfed by Chicago's lofty skyscrapers. *Photo by Kee Chang, Chicago Association of Commerce and Industry.*

8

Chicago

It has been called the most American of cities. It has been called many other things, too. "A gargantuan and inordinate abattoir," wrote H. L. Mencken. "City of the broad shoulders," caroled Carl Sandburg. Rudyard Kipling paid a visit and remarked later: "Having seen it I urgently desire never to see it again. It is inhabited by savages." Yet another poet advised us to "bet your bottom dollar you'll lose your blues" in that toddlin' town.

It survived massacre, fire, and Al Capone. It hosted the Republican Convention of 1860, in which Abraham Lincoln was nominated for the presidency, and the Democratic Convention of 1968, when police and demonstrators were bloodied in streets reeking of tear gas. It contains some of the country's most squalid slums, the wealth of the Gold Coast, and the most distinguished architecture and urban planning ever assayed on this continent. It contains one of the most impressive collections of museums anywhere, a symphony orchestra ranked among the world's best, and a baseball team that once threw the World Series. In seventy years it grew from a collection of huts on the prairie to America's second city. During a time of urban despair, it was known as "the city that works," although its mayor was described as running one of the country's most corrupt political machines.

The most American of cities, to be sure. It was really never anything else. It had no colonial past, no long foreign associations. Only a brief brush with French fur traders and missionaries marked its development until a small American garrison arrived after the Revolutionary War. The French, in the early years of western exploration, recognized the value of the site occupied by a large village of Potawatomis. The easy portage there between Lake Michigan and the Des Plaines River was the fastest route from the Great Lakes to the Mississippi. This portage was discovered by Louis Joliet and Fr. Jacques Marquette on the return leg of their voyage to the Upper Mississippi in 1673. Marquette became the first European to live in the area when he returned the following winter and was trapped there by ice. He settled in, became ill, and died the following spring as he attempted to return to his home mission in St. Ignace, Michigan. The portage was used by later explorers on their way south, notably Robert LaSalle, and by 1696 there was a permanent mission in the area under Fr. Francois Pinet.

But the French, who had run afoul of the Iroquois Confederacy in the eastern Great Lakes, had the same trouble with the Fox in the west. The Fox objected to France's alliance with the Sioux, and by 1702 they had forced abandonment of the mission at the portage. During the remainder of the eighteenth century, Chicago was a wilderness, with only an occasional trader or Indian band breaking the silence of the prairie.

The Illinois Territory entered American hands during the Revolutionary War, but British control was not removed from the area until 1796, when United States forces entered Detroit. This opened up the Northwest to the young republic, and it was decided that a string of forts should be established at other strategic points along the western lakes. They would act as a check on lingering British ambitions in the area. Accordingly, in the summer of 1803 Captain John Whistler and a command of sixty-six soldiers were sent across Michigan to erect Fort Dearborn on the bend of the Chicago River near the lake. (This bend has been altered, as has the very direction of the river's flow. Today the river continues straight ahead into the lake instead of curving south, and flows backwards from the lake.)

The military soon was joined by John Kinzie, a Quebec-born trader who settled in with his family. Later generations regarded him as the father of Chicago. The fort remained an isolated frontier post, troubled by frequent internal bickering and sporadic clashes with the surrounding tribes. Then in the summer of 1812 came disturbing news. Reports came in that Fort Mackinac had fallen to the British and that Britain's Indian allies were up in arms. Captain Nathan Heald, the fort commandant, was ordered to withdraw to safety. On the morning of August 15, the garrison and civilian traders and their families rode from the fort with two supply wagons. They advanced about a mile and a half (to the vicinity of Calumet Avenue and Eighteenth Street on today's map) when Indians appeared from behind the sand dunes along the lake and attacked. Thirty-eight soldiers, two women, and twelve children, including an unborn baby ripped from its mother's womb, were slaughtered. Kinzie and Heald escaped, and friendly Potawatomi helped other survivors to safety. The bones of the fallen lay among the dunes for four years until Americans finally returned to the area to bury them.

The garrison resumed operation in 1816, but fourteen years later Chicago was still nothing more than half a dozen log houses and the fort. Yet when Illinois became a state in 1818 its Congressman, Nathanael Pope, insisted that boundaries established by the Northwest Ordinance be altered to attach Chicago to the new state. (Under the 1787 ordinance, the area should have belonged to Wisconsin—a fact that was pointed out quite bitterly by that state when it joined the union thirty years after Illinois.) Pope pointed out that, without this port, Illinois would surely be dominated by southern economic interests and inevitably become a slave state. He foresaw the lake port coming to control the entire trade of the Northwest and becoming the major city of the region. Pope, however, was in the minority. Early travelers turned in mixed reports on the potential of the area. Bankers in booming Shawneetown, an Illinois metropolis on the Ohio River, turned down a loan request from the settlement on the grounds that it had no prospects. Chicago was platted in 1830, and its squatter residents were offered land at $35 a lot. Kinzie's family bought 102 acres north of the river and passed up the chance for more. Not many others were even that interested. When Chicago officially became a city in 1833, land in what is now the Loop sold for $6.72 an acre.

The outbreak of another Indian scare, the Black Hawk War of 1832, gave Chicago the boost it needed. Settlers who had trickled into northern Illinois retreated in panic to Fort Dearborn as Sauks raided out of Iowa Territory to reclaim their land. A relief force from Detroit was stricken with cholera en route on the lake. Only one ship made it in and its troops were too sick to fight. Nonetheless, the war was over by the end of summer. Soldiers involved in the brief campaign carried the word back east that good land was available in Illinois. Gen. Winfield Scott, who led the United States forces, advised Congress to build a harbor in Chicago. The rush was on. By 1837 the population was 4,000, and a grid of streets was optimistically laid out to encompass a city of ten square miles.

Slowly Chicago was becoming the transportation hub of the new West. When President James Polk vetoed a river and harbor bill in 1846, many western states held a convention in Chicago and pledged to work for federal improvements in internal commerce. Chicago was at the center of these programs. A canal to the Mississippi was finished in 1848; four years later the railroad arrived from Detroit. By 1856 four rail lines converged in Chicago. They led south to Cairo and west to Rock Island and Quincy. Chicago was now a city of 93,000, economic center of the state that furnished both major presidential candidates in the pivotal 1860 election. Through the Great Lakes and the Erie Canal, Chicago was tied to the east and Atlantic trade. After the Civil War it was linked again—through its canal to the Mississippi—with the South and the Gulf ports. By 1870 it was a booming metropolis of 300,000 people and the economic center of the American interior, as Pope foresaw half a century before.

The great fire of the following year is part of folklore, a famous disaster that lives on in myth as well as history. Recitation of the losses is astonishing enough: 17,000 buildings; 100,000 homeless; $200 million in property; 300 dead. The October blaze was part of a chain of fires that swept across the lakes from Wisconsin to the Lake Huron shore of Michigan. The other fires of that deadly autumn are nearly forgotten. Chicago's remains bracketed with the San Francisco earthquake as a calamity of the ages.

The fire began in Patrick O'Leary's barn, near Halsted and Twelfth streets, at 9:00 P.M. on October 8, a Sunday evening. When it finally burned itself out early Tuesday morning near the northern city limits at Fullerton Avenue, the entire business district was in ruins, as were most of Chicago's warehouses, mansions, brothels, and government offices. In a few days, however, the rebirth was already under way. "Cheer Up" headlined the *Chicago Tribune* in a front page editorial. Relief funds poured in from across the country. Civic boosters headed east telling young men of vision that now was the time to make a fortune in a revived Chicago. Grant Park was formed by refuse from the burned-out business district dumped into the lake.

The new city was built by men who already had made their fortunes. It rose on a grander scale, on a stage swept clean of the city's rude beginnings. In twenty years Chicago was holding the Columbian Exposition, a world's fair that would reshape American ideas on urban beauty and city planning. Louis Sullivan and the Chicago school of architects were inventing the skyscraper and changing the look of every city in the country. Daniel Burnham, head architect of the Columbian Exposition, drew up the Chicago Plan of 1909 that would remake the lakefront into one of the most striking urban settings in the world. "Make no little plans," wrote Burnham. "They have no magic to stir men's blood." The Chicago of travel posters and picture postcards today is mostly the result of Burnham's big plans.

Chicago remains the hub of the Great Lakes. Its airport is the busiest in the world, its halls and hotels full of conventioneers, its night life raucous, its cultural facilities superb. It has the sense of open space that New York lacks, the central core not found in Los Angeles, a stability unknown in Houston, the grace missing from Detroit. Chicago is the most American city—and in many ways the best.

The Loop

The skyscraper was invented in Chicago, pushed upwards by inventive architects who experimented with new materials and forms in the decade after the great fire. It was also in Chicago that the style reached its fullest realization. On this walk you will pass the world's oldest surviving steel-frame skyscraper, as well as the world's tallest. You will see how urban planners are trying to lighten the steep steel canyons by providing open spaces centered around works of art. Any stroll in central Chicago invariably turns into an architecture lesson, but this one is the basic text on the subject.

Most outsiders use *the Loop* as a term synonymous with downtown Chicago. Historically, though, *the Loop* refers to the area enclosed by the elevated railway, the old business core of the city south of the Chicago River. Most of this walk winds through the quadrilateral formed by the elevated system.

It begins, however, in Grant Park, which is east of the Loop on ground that once was lake bottom. Buckingham Fountain, the focus of the park, is situated amid pedestrian paths that are the continuation of Congress Street beyond Michigan Avenue. Grant Park was included in Daniel Burnham's Chicago Plan of 1909, but had been protected before that by a most unlikely champion, A. Montgomery Ward. The millionaire merchant was described by the *Chicago Tribune* at the turn of the century as "a human icicle, shunning and shunned in all but the relations of business." But Ward was outraged that commercial buildings had cut off the lake side of Michigan Avenue in defiance of an ordinance passed in 1837. Ward fought in the courts for thirteen years to have the structures torn down and the lakeside preserved as parkland for the city. "Here is a park frontage on the lake," argued Ward, "comparing favorably with the Bay of Naples, which city officials would crowd with buildings, transforming the breathing spot for the poor into a showground of the educated rich. I do not think it is right." He won the battle in 1903; and every building, with the exception of the Art Institute of Chicago, came down. "Perhaps," said Ward, "I may see the public appreciate my efforts. But I doubt it."

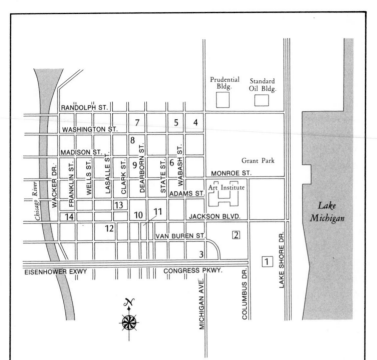

1 Buckingham Fountain
2 Lincoln Statue
3 Auditorium Building
4 Chicago Cultural Center
5 Marshall Fields
6 Carson Pirie Scott
7 Daley Plaza
8 Chicago Temple
9 First National Plaza
10 Federal Center
11 Monadnock Building
12 Board of Trade
13 The Rookery
14 Sears Tower

A Walk through the Loop

Nevertheless, the park concept had been established and Burnham was able to persuade the city to fill in the lake from its natural shore at Michigan Avenue all the way to its present boundary beyond Outer Drive. The Clarence Buckingham Fountain was opened in 1927, built with a $750,000 bequest by Kate Buckingham as a memorial to her brother. (Miss Buckingham, one of the city's most generous art patrons, had inherited a large fortune based in grain elevators.) The fountain was modeled after one in the Gardens of Versailles, but is more than twice the size of the original. Its mechanism has 133 jets capable of using 14,000 gallons of water a minute. At full blast, water from the center jet can attain a height of 200 feet. The fountain operates from May 20 through September 30, from 11:30 A.M. to 3:00 P.M. and from 5:00 P.M. to 9:00 P.M. There is a nightly color display from 9:00 to 10:00, and on concert evenings in Grant Park the time is extended to 10:30. In July and August there is an additional midday display from 12:30 to 1:00.

Head west from the fountain and after crossing Columbus Drive look to your right for the Lincoln statue, the last work of sculptor Augustus Saint-Gaudens. Beyond the seated Lincoln are the bridge over the Illinois Central tracks and the Indian horsemen, created by Ivan Mestrovic, that guard the entrance to the park. Across the street is the solid wall of buildings that looms over the park from Polk Street on the south to the park's northern extremity at Randolph Street. The precipice of concrete, glass, and steel opposite the wide expanse of park is a stunning spectacle, much like the Rampart range of the Rockies rising sheer from the Colorado plains.

A venerable Chicago hotel dating from 1893, the Pick-Congress, stands on the south side of Congress Street. On the north is one of architect Louis Sullivan's greatest triumphs, the Auditorium Building. Its opening in 1889 was regarded as an event significant enough for President Benjamin Harrison to be in attendance. Harrison was criticized because the Auditorium was, in fact, a private building, but he responded to his Chicago audience: "Such criticism springs from those who have never seen your great buildings." This building was indeed something to see. Sullivan had combined with engineer Denkmar Adler on a commission from socialite Ferdinand Wythe Peck to build the finest auditorium in the country. It was the first to be constructed with acoustics rather than sight lines as the major consideration. Furthermore, it contained only forty private boxes, a major change in opera house design; Peck felt such privilege should be regarded with "infinite scorn and patriotic dislike." Surrounding the auditorium itself were a hotel and offices. At its opening a crowd of 20,000 lined the streets outside trying to catch a glimpse of the interior. The building's ownership went bankrupt in 1940 and was taken over by Roosevelt University six years later. The theatre, however, was left untouched and, after a generation of darkness, was reopened in 1967 with $2.25 million worth of restorations. The lobby may be seen during regular weekday business hours. Its rich ornamentation, devised by Sullivan and Adler, makes a visit worthwhile. Concerts are scheduled throughout the year, and the university also conducts tours of the auditorium. For hours and details, call 922-2110.

Turn north on Michigan. The Chicago School of Architecture Foundation has dubbed this section of the avenue the "Splendid Mile," to contrast with the "Magnificent Mile" built a generation later on the north side of the river. Between Congress and Randolph, the avenue is lined with historic and prestigious buildings. Especially noteworthy on the way are Orchestra Hall, at 220 South Michigan, home of the Chicago Symphony and designed by Burnham in 1905; the Gage Building, at 18 South Michigan, a Louis Sullivan work of 1898, cited by the Chicago Landmarks Commission for its inspired ornamentation; and the Tower Building, at 6 North Michigan, formerly the offices of Montgomery Ward. It was from here that the firm's crusty chairman cast a cold eye on the structures obscuring his lake view across the street and began the battle for Grant Park.

At the corner of Washington Street you will have an unobstructed view of the two great towers at the northern limit of the park, the Prudential Building and the Standard Oil Building. You may want to take the short walk over to them to admire the pool and *Standing Sculpture* by Harry Bertoia in front of the Standard building (the taller of the two.) That building is eighty stories and 1,136 feet high. If you choose simply to admire from a distance, continue the walk by turning left and entering the building on the north side of Washington, the Chicago Public Library Cultural Center. The block-long structure was put up in 1897 and renovated eighty years later, after its stacks of books were removed and its function changed. The Louis Tiffany dome above the Washington entrance is one of its major attractions, as are the marble staircases and the mosaics on the walls and ceiling. Besides the appeal of the building itself, there are exhibits relating to Chicago history or culture.

Walk through the Center and exit on Randolph Street. Turn left, then left again at Wabash Street, the first block. You are now right below the elevated tracks that mark the beginning of the Loop proper. Right across the street is the main entrance to Marshall Fields, the city's largest department store. Between 1892 and 1914 it gradually expanded on this site to fill the entire block. After a look inside, continue south on Wabash to Madison Street and turn right. For map enthusiasts, the store just across Madison is a treasure house. It is the home office of Rand McNally and Company, one of the country's largest repositories of maps and charts.

Continue to the corner of State Street. On the southeastern side is another of Chicago's great department stores and architectural landmarks, Carson Pirie Scott and Company. The building is one of Sullivan's most famous works, one that turns up in all the texts on American architecture. Sullivan's structure, built in two stages between 1899 and 1904, covers the area around the State-Madison intersection. Later additions extend south on State, remaining true to the spirit of the original. Notice in particular the horizontally elongated windows, the "Chicago windows" that were a hallmark of Sullivan's thinking on the treatment of light. Look also for the rich ornamentation of the facade, which manages not to detract from the overall strength and discipline of the building.

Now turn right on State and follow it for one block back to Washington. On the southwest corner is 32 North State, another building cited by the Chicago Landmarks Commission for its pioneering use of glass. It was designed by Burnham's firm in

1895, although its materials make it seem far more contemporary than that.

Continue left on Washington for one block to Dearborn Street. The open plaza in front of you sets off the Richard J. Daley Center, an assemblage of city and county offices named for the late engineer of the Cook County Democratic machine. More arresting than the building, however, is the sculpture in front of it, known simply as the Chicago Picasso. Chicago has never been a great respecter of reputation, and when the great artist donated this sculpture to the city it was accepted with equal measures of gratitude and derision. Newspapers ran contests to try and guess what it was, while others marveled at the power of the fifty-foot-high artwork. After a decade in place, though, it has become a civic institution. Both building and sculpture are made of Cor-Ten steel, which oxidized over the years to its present brownish hue.

Across from the plaza's southwestern corner is the Chicago Temple, which claims to be the tallest church building in the world. Home of the First United Methodist Church, founded in 1831, the office building extends 551 feet to the tip of its Gothic spire. The building was completed in 1924. Tours of the church and the Chapel in the Sky (at the 400-foot level) are given at 2:00, Monday through Saturday, and at 10:30 and 12:15 on Sunday.

Return to Dearborn and turn right. This section of Dearborn contains two more of Chicago's outdoor artworks, compositions by Marc Chagall and Alexander Calder. The Chagall comes first, in the plaza of the First National Bank Building south of Madison. *The Four Seasons* is a massive 3,000-square-foot mosaic, 70 feet long, 14 feet high, illuminated by 350 different shades of stone and glass that change tone with the angle of the sun. At a lower level behind the Chagall is a larger plaza and a fountain of nine water columns. The bank building itself is a powerful **A**-shaped structure completed in 1969. It is sixty stories high. Just across Dearborn is another of the city's notable modern towers, the Inland Steel Building, one of the first to use glass and steel as primary materials. It was put up in 1957 by Skidmore, Owings, and Merrill.

Continue south on Dearborn for another two blocks to the third of the great open plazas, the Federal Center. The center actually occupies both sides of the street, with the Everett Dirksen Building on the east and the post office and John C. Kluczynski Building on the west. The grouping was executed by Mies van der Rohe. In the center of the plaza on the west side is *Flamingo,* a fifty-three-foot-high Calder stabile painted an especially vivid shade of red.

Turn right at Jackson Boulevard, the next corner, and once more you're back at the very beginning of the skyscraper era. The Monadnock Building, constructed between 1891 and 1893, was a sensation at its opening. It was then the largest office building in the world (a title now held by the Sears Tower, which you will encounter in a little while). At sixteen stories and 197 feet in height it is still an impressive, powerful structure. The Monadnock was the first building to use the floating foundation, a steel and concrete underground raft, to stabilize high-rises in Chicago's swampy ground. The building also was the site of tests taken during a gale that proved to skeptics that the new skyscrapers were stable enough to withstand high winds—an attribute that was by no means taken for granted in the nineteenth century.

Continue along Jackson, across Clark Street, to the foot of LaSalle Street. There, in an art deco building topped by a statue of Ceres, the Greek goddess of grain, is the Board of Trade. Make it a point to arrive before 1:00 P.M. on a weekday for admission to the visitor's gallery of the Trading Room. It opens at 9:30 A.M., Monday through Friday. There is no admission charge. The scene of utter chaos unfolding on the floor below is actually the workings of the largest commodities futures market in the world. Although there are guides, pamphlets, and a movie to help explain what is going on, it is all a bit incomprehensible. Nevertheless, the frantic action, movement, and noise make it a most exciting panorama, one of the most remarkable experiences in Chicago. Time your walk to ensure that you will arrive when the gallery is open.

The two massive structures on either side of LaSalle outside the front door of the Board of Trade represent the focus of the financial district. On the right is the Continental Illinois National

Bank; on the left the Federal Reserve Bank for the Midwest. Power is the unmistakable theme of these monoliths, and the message is conveyed precisely. Continue north on the eastern side of LaSalle to a more winning building, a pioneer skyscraper with the beguiling sobriquet of the Rookery. This building at 209 South LaSalle was finished in 1886 and is the oldest steel skeleton skyscraper in the world. It replaced a temporary city hall—built after the great fire—that had become a favorite gathering place for pigeons and so was popularly known as the Rookery. The newer building inherited the site and the name. The exterior remains impressive after a century, but the Rookery's real attraction is its lobby, designed by Frank Lloyd Wright in 1905. It is a jewelbox of gold and ivory decor. Examine the grillwork along the balconies and cylindrical staircase. The Rookery was also one of the first buildings to use its lobby as an interior square for shops and offices.

You've been walking a long time, but the end is in sight. It has been in sight for most of the way, since you're headed for the Sears Tower, the tallest office building in the world. It offers a view of Chicago that is, quite truthfully, unsurpassed. Turn left on Adams Street from the Rookery, pass beneath the western limit of the Loop, cross Franklin Street, and there it is—all 110 stories (1,454 feet) and 4.5 million square feet of it. National headquarters of Sears, Roebuck and Company is located on the first fifty floors. A working population of 16,500 people is absorbed daily in the building, which was completed in 1974. There is a mechanized Calder mural, *Universe,* in the lobby; but the big show here is the view from the top, the Skydeck. The viewpoint at the 1,353-foot level on the 103rd floor is open daily from 9:00 A.M. to midnight. There is an admission charge. From here the route you have just walked can be examined at leisure, as can the entire metropolitan area. On clear days the view extends for fifty miles—as far as Kenosha, Wisconsin, to the north, clear across Lake Michigan to the state of Michigan on the east. The Rookery, the tiny building that was the distant ancestor of this proud tower, is almost lost in the shadows far below.

To the Gold Coast

Chicago is constantly making itself over. In the years after the great fire, then in the 1920s as Burnham's Chicago Plan went into effect, and again during the tremendous construction boom of the 1960s, the face of the city changed tremendously. Yet much remains the same, giving Chicago a certain sense of stability and charm that makes it a livable, human city. This walk will take you to parts of the city that have changed completely in the last half century, and some areas that look much as they did 100 years ago.

The walk starts at Dearborn Street and Wacker Drive, on the south side of the Chicago River. Wacker itself is a prime example of the changes undertaken in the 1920s. This double-decked highway that follows the contours of the river was once a hopeless tangle of stalls and vendors, the South Water Street Market. In 1925 the market was shut down and construction of this new artery around the Loop was begun. At its completion, Mayor William E. Dever hailed it as "a miracle," which was no overstatement to those familiar with its former impassable state. The drive was named for Charles Wacker, a vigorous advocate of various aspects of the Chicago Plan, including this one.

Directly across the river is a symbol of the Chicago that began taking shape in the 1960s. The scalloped cylinders of Marina City became one of Chicago's most familiar images after their completion in 1964. The towers, which house residential apartments, are of concrete slab construction, at sixty-two stories the highest such structures in Chicago. You can enter the complex by crossing the Dearborn Street bridge. A model apartment is always on display. (The bridge itself was named the most beautiful steel movable span in the country by the American Institute of Steel Construction. A marker on the walkway says so.)

Continue along Wacker for one block to Heald Square, an open space in the midst of a skyscraper thicket. The square is named for the commander of the ill-fated evacuation of Fort Dearborn in 1812. In its center is a sculptured group of Revolutionary War heroes that must brighten the hearts of Chicago's financiers as they pass by daily. It shows George Washington flanked by the two moneymen behind the colonial efforts, Haym

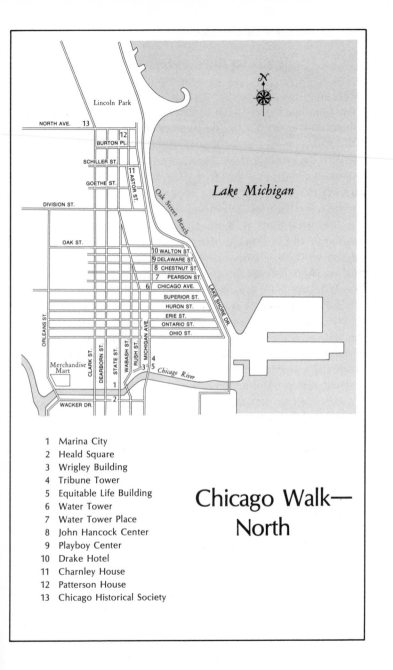

1   Marina City
2   Heald Square
3   Wrigley Building
4   Tribune Tower
5   Equitable Life Building
6   Water Tower
7   Water Tower Place
8   John Hancock Center
9   Playboy Center
10 Drake Hotel
11 Charnley House
12 Patterson House
13 Chicago Historical Society

Chicago Walk— North

Salomon and Robert Morris. On the south side of the square is the striking Seventeenth Church of Christ Scientist, a dome-shaped edifice completed in 1968. Another distinctive building is the slender needle of the Lincoln Tower, a twenty-four-story structure with the smallest space per floor of any Chicago skyscraper. Heald Square is also the perfect place for viewing the concentration of buildings across the river, from Marina City to the Gothic spires of the Tribune Tower (which we'll come to shortly).

As you reach the Michigan Avenue bridge you are standing on the site of Fort Dearborn, a fact attested to by about a dozen plaques in the vicinity. Looking across the bridge you can see the double-deck arrangement on North Michigan and Wacker. In theory, it clears traffic by shunting heavy trucks through the area below street level. How efficiently it actually works may be observed at any rush hour.

Two of Chicago's most famous buildings lie right across the bridge on either side of Michigan, guarding the entrance to the Magnificent Mile. On the west is the Wrigley Building, dating from 1921. It is actually two towers joined by a bridge. Its white exterior, clock tower, and nightly illumination make it one of the most conspicuous features of the Chicago skyline. Across the street is the Tribune Tower, an attempt to apply Gothic architecture, complete with flying buttresses, to the skyscraper. This landmark was completed in 1925 after *Tribune* publisher Robert R. McCormick had held an international competition for its design. Tours of Chicago's largest newspaper are given Monday through Friday at 9:30, 11:00, 1:15 and 2:45; Saturday at 9:30, noon, and 1:15. The tours are free, but reservations must be made in advance by calling 222-3993.

A more contemporary structure occupies the angle lying between the Tribune Tower and the river. The Equitable Life Building, a forty-story metal and glass structure emblematic of the city's more recent style in skyscrapers, was completed in 1965. The building is set off by another of Chicago's great plazas, Pioneer Court, an open area that features a fountain with the names of Chicago's first "first families" around the base. A flight of stairs leads to shops and cafes at river level.

Turn back to the Tribune Tower for a fast world tour. McCormick, always on the alert for the grand gesture, decided to link his new building with the ages by embedding chunks of other historic structures in its exterior limestone. So there, clearly labeled around the street level facade, are pieces of the Colosseum of Rome, the Great Wall of China, the Great Pyramid, and dozens of other unlikely spots.

The Tribune Tower is the start of the Magnificent Mile, the stretch of North Michigan Avenue that includes most of the city's fashionable shops and hotels. The avenue was widened in the 1920s and, in effect, extended central Chicago north from the river to Oak Street, where Michigan Avenue ends at the lake. It is an area for strolling, window shopping, and enjoying the city at a slower pace than the tempo prevailing in the Loop. Most of the buildings here date from the 1920s or later—with one notable exception. As you proceed up the avenue you will see it in front of you: the stone turrets of the Water Tower. This strange structure was the city's symbol of survival after the fire of 1871. In the haunting photographs taken the day after the fire, the tower stands alone amid smoking ruins and stunned residents, looking then just as it does one century later. Michigan Avenue even jogs slightly in the tower's vicinity to avoid disturbing it. It was completed in 1869, an ersatz Gothic curiosity that gave no clue to its actual function. It ceased long ago to have any connection with the city water system, but its symbolic meaning is far more important.

On the next block up Michigan Avenue, after Pearson Street, is one of Chicago's proudest new monuments, a striking high-rise shopping mall and luxury hotel. When it came time to choose a name for this development, the inevitable selection was Water Tower Place, giving the new kid on the block immediate identity with the doughty landmark it overshadows. Water Tower Place, completed in 1976, transfers the suburban shopping mall into an urban framework. Seven floors of shops are built around a vast central atrium, complete with splashing fountains and glass-enclosed elevators. Marshall Fields and Lord and Taylor anchor the retail development, with 100 other shops filling in the remaining space. It is Chicago's distinctive answer to providing suburban amenities in a wholly urban setting. Canadian cities have responded to the same problem by building underground; Chicago characteristically went straight up. Atop the shopping mall is the Ritz-Carlton Hotel, occupying floors twelve to sixty-two of the tower (with prices to match the elevation).

One block north is the tallest tower in the neighborhood, the John Hancock Center, or "Big John" to its admirers. At one hundred stories and 1,030 feet, the Hancock Center was an immediate Chicago favorite. The giant **X**'s formed by its steel crossbracings and its setting, somewhat apart from the city's other giant high-rises, make it Chicago's most easily identifiable building. Completed in 1969, the center is part office building and part apartment house, with residences on the top fifty floors. If you took the first walk in this book you already went up to the taller Sears Tower for the view. But the vantage point atop the Hancock Center, looking right up the lakeshore, also repays the elevator fare. The observatory is open daily from 9:00 A.M. to midnight.

On the next block north is the Playboy Center, taking in what was once the Palmolive Building and the Knickerbocker Hotel. It is headquarters for the Playboy Corporation which began its publishing and pleasure-seeking empire in Chicago. The center is an exciting blend of two of Chicago's most dynamic architectural periods. Stroll through the lobby arcade to see the stunning effects accomplished in the 1972 remodeling of the 1920s structures.

The Drake Hotel, for many years the most prestigious in the city, overlooks the lake at the corner of Michigan and Oak. From here a tunnel leads beneath Lake Shore Drive to parks and beaches, and to the luxury apartments of the Gold Coast rising to the west. Instead we'll turn left on Oak, past an attractive area of small shops, theaters, and restaurants. Turn right on Rush Street, the city's nightclub strip, where a variety of establishments endeavor to separate conventioneers from their cash as swiftly and painlessly as possible. Rush soon merges with State Street. Continue north, then turn right on Division Street. The first street you come to is Astor, designated a landmark area for its entire six-block course by the Chicago Landmarks Commission. Turn left and start walking. You are entering a delightful area where, with barely a false note, nineteenth-century mansions and town-houses mingle with 1970s high-rise apartments. It is a lovingly preserved piece of history, exemplifying how Chicago has managed to keep the best of its past in the midst of a booming present. The combination makes the entire near North Side one of the most vital urban areas in America. A walk down Astor displays some of the best of it.

There are two buildings of special note on the way. The first, at the southeastern corner of Astor and Schiller streets, is Charnley House. The firm of Sullivan and Adler has been credited with construction of this 1892 single-family home, but it is actually one of the earliest surviving works of Frank Lloyd Wright. At the northwestern corner of Astor and Burton Place is the Patterson House, built by New York architect Stanford White in 1900. It was commissioned for the daughter of *Chicago Tribune* editor Joseph Medill and was later owned by the Cyrus McCormick family. In its time it was the city's toniest address, with visiting royalty often housed within by their wealthy hosts.

Astor ends at North Avenue at the southern edge of Lincoln Park. The walk can end here; but if this stroll through a portion of the Gold Coast has raised an appetite for Chicago's past, simply turn left for three more blocks. At the corner of North and Clark Street is the Chicago Historical Society. This museum devoted to local history has excellent displays on pioneer life, the great fire, and Abraham Lincoln. Just as evocative is a hall containing the wardrobes of nineteenth-century Chicago's grandest dames, the leaders of society in the era before World War I. The display enables you to get a sense of what the Gold Coast looked like inside those splendid Astor Street addresses. The museum is open Monday through Saturday, 9:30 to 4:30; Sunday, noon to 5:00. There is an admission charge.

The Great Museums

One measure of Chicago's strength is its museums. It has five institutions that rank with the world's finest in their fields. Moreover, they represent a civic leadership that cared enough about its city to pour in the funds and energy to create and operate them. They are as much a record of Chicago's colorful history and of the people who shaped the face of the city as they are great museums. The five we'll visit are: the Museum of Science and Industry, on the far-flung South Side; the Art Institute of Chicago, on the fringe of the Loop; and a group of three institutions in Burnham Park, just south of the central business district—Field Museum of Natural History, the John G. Shedd Aquarium, and the Adler Planetarium.

The oldest is the Art Institute, guarded by its powerful bronze lions that gaze out over Michigan Avenue. The Institute was built in 1892 on what then was the lakeshore. It was the only building on the east side of Michigan to be exempted from the court order that cleared all structures from the area in 1903. Prior to the opening of this building, its collection was a paltry grab-bag of a few Old Masters and lots of plaster casts. Then two wealthy members of Chicago pioneer families decided to rectify the situation. Martin Ryerson and Charles L. Hutchinson applied the wide-awake business practices of their hometown to the art world. Ryerson is credited with outmaneuvering a European museum for one panel by the unheard-of expedient of rising earlier than his competitors and getting to the dealer with the morning sun. Ryerson was the scholar, Hutchinson the fundraiser. Between them they managed to convince Chicago's social elite to put up staggering sums of money for art. When a Florentine prince sold his collection, Hutchinson raced to Italy with $200,000 in hand and acquired fifteen Flemish masterworks. Ryerson is credited with being the first American collector to acquire El Grecos, years before the Spanish artist came back into fashion. The museum still is regarded as having the country's leading collection of El Grecos, as well as an outstanding assortment of French Impressionists, Post-Impressionists, and Rembrandts. Its collection of Oriental and primitive art is also highly regarded. Among its more recent acquisitions are the stained glass *American Windows* by Marc Chagall and the reconstructed trading room of the Chicago Stock Exchange Building (one of Louis Sullivan's finest, demolished in 1972). The Institute is open daily. Hours are Monday through Saturday, 10:00 to 5:00, except Thursday when closing is extended to 8:00 P.M.; Sunday, noon to 5:00. There is an admission charge, except on Thursday.

The building housing the Museum of Science and Industry in Jackson Park dates from one year after the Art Institute was built. It was originally the Fine Arts Building of the Columbian Exposition, a huge world's fair honoring the 400th anniversary of Christopher Columbus's American landing. Uncharacteristically for Chicago, the fair opened one year late in 1893. The Exposition carried its chief planner, Daniel Burnham, to national fame and gave him the platform from which he launched the Chicago Plan to remake this native city. But Sullivan, another member of the Exposition planning board, was less than delighted with the whole affair. He wanted the architecture of the fair to reflect the development of the Chicago school. Burnham, bowing to eastern pressure, decided on a classical motif. "This will set architecture in this country back by half a century," grumped Sullivan. His own Transportation Building in the contemporary style was one of the hits of the fair, though. The two biggest smashes, however, were the first ferris wheel in America and the hoochy-coochy danced on the Midway by Little Egypt. The Exposition also is credited with earning Chicago its most enduring nickname. In 1889, when several cities were competing for the fair, New York newspaper editor Charles A. Dana scoffed at the pretensions of the rival in the west. "Pay no attention to the nonsensical claims of that windy city," wrote Dana. "Its people could not build a World's Fair even if they won it." The Windy City did hold the fair, though, just twenty-two years after being leveled by the great fire, and it was a landmark of the city's history.

Today the museum attracts more than three million visitors annually. So compelling are its displays that each visitor stays an average of three and a half hours. It takes much more than a day to see the museum; even a weekend is barely adequate. There are 2,000 displays in seventy-five halls over fourteen acres of floor space. The exhibits are so diverse and plentiful, it's hard to know where to begin. The most popular, according to museum officials, are a working coal mine, a captured German submarine, the daily hatching of chicks, and actress Colleen Moore's Fairy Castle dollhouse. Corporations sponsor displays showing the latest advances in every conceivable field—from computers to medicine. There is an Apollo-space capsule, a sixteen-foot-high model of a human heart, and miniature railroads. Visitors are invited to participate by pushing buttons or turning cranks that activate the machinery, or by taking computer quizzes that test their knowledge on things like health and nutrition.

Yet for over ten years of its existence this handsome facility sat vacant and decaying. As the Fine Arts Building of the exposition it was intended to incorporate features of several temples on the Acropolis in Athens. The Field Museum of Natural History moved in after the fair closed. But when that museum moved to its present home in 1920, the Jackson Park building was abandoned. Meanwhile, Julius Rosenwald, president of Sears, Roebuck, was looking for a location to house a new museum of technology in Chicago. He put up one million dollars to that end, but found no takers. In 1925, however, Chicago voters approved a five million dollar bond issue to rehabilitate the old Fine Arts Building. Rosenwald upped his contribution to three million dollars, and the Museum of Science and Industry was born. It opened in 1933, in conjunction with Chicago's second world's fair, the Century of Progress, although work on the building was not completed until 1940. Today the museum is Chicago's most popular attraction, the best of its kind anywhere. It is probably the one "can't miss" sight in the city. Admission and parking are free, although there is a small charge for some exhibits. The museum is open Monday through Friday, 9:30 to 4:00 and to 5:30 from May through Labor Day. Weekend hours are 9:30 to 5:30.

One of the key elements of Burnham's Chicago Plan involved pushing back the lakefront to the east and filling in the former bottomland with parks. The first structure to rise on this reclaimed land was the Field Museum of Natural History, started in 1911. Nine years later the collections were moved there from Jackson Park, and the first of the Burnham Park museums was in business. Exhibits in the Field Museum are grouped according to scientific discipline—anthropology, botany, geology, and zoology. Branching off from its enormous skylighted entrance hall are forty-two display areas and six major galleries. The museum is famous for its primitive art collection, its dioramas showing mounted animals as they appear in their natural habitat, its Hall of Gems, its displays of Man and His Environment, and the Place of Wonder, where visitors may handle the exhibits. Its biggest crowd-pleaser, though, always has been the Hall of Dinosaurs, with its rows of skeletons of the giant prehistoric reptiles. The museum is open Monday through Thursday and on weekends, 9:00 to 6:00 in summer, 9:00 to 4:00 in winter, and 9:00 to 5:00 the rest of the year. On winter weekends, hours are extended to 5:00. On Friday, the year-round hours are 9:00 to 9:00. There is an admission charge, except on Friday.

The area south of the museum, extending along both sides of the Yacht Basin lagoon, was the site of the great Century of Progress Exhibition in 1933, celebrating Chicago's centennial as a city. It was held forty years after the Columbian Exposition, but tastes change slowly. Just like its predecessor, the fair's biggest draws were a spectacular ride and a dancer. The Sky Ride, which carried passengers high above the basin, was billed as the transportation system of the future, moving people between cities in elevated cable cars. The dancer, Sally Rand, had more staying power. She was still performing her famous fan dance until her death in 1979.

Many visitors to the fair also found the time to visit the two recently opened museums in the area. The Shedd Aquarium had been completed in 1929 and the Adler Planetarium two years later. The aquarium, named for the chairman of the board of Marshall Fields, is the largest such facility in the world. It has an underwater population of 7,500 housed in 130 tanks. Most spectacular is the 90,000-gallon reef tank, in which a Caribbean underwater community is recreated complete with 350 colorful tropical fish. A diver enters the tank at 11:00 and 2:00 daily to feed the inhabitants. The aquarium is open Saturday through

Thursday, 10:00 to 4:00, in winter; in summer, 9:00 to 6:00; rest of the year, 10:00 to 5:00. It is open Friday all year, 9:00 to 9:00. There is an admission charge, except on Friday.

Spectacular views of the Chicago lakefront and skyline open up from the causeway that connects the aquarium and planetarium. They are two blocks apart, and it is a stroll to take slowly. The Adler Planeterium, named for a former vice president of Sears, Roebuck, was the first built in the Western Hemisphere. The facility includes a museum of astronomy, with antique instruments, exhibits on telescope making, and Apollo lunar landing craft. The big show, though, is the Sky Theater, where the giant Zeiss projector reproduces the night sky for viewers. The show is combined with multi-media displays in the Universe Theater and, on clear summer nights, with a visit to the Doane Observatory, where a television monitor attached to a sixteen-inch telescope shows magnified views of distant space. The museum is open from 9:30 to 4:30, Monday through Thursday; to 5:00 on weekends; and to 9:30 on Friday. From mid-June through August it is open daily, 9:30 A.M. to 9:00 P.M. Planetarium shows are scheduled throughout the day.

Other Things to See

[1]   Sheridan Road winds from the Wisconsin line to the North Side of Chicago, with many views of the lake and the stately homes of suburban Chicago on the way. It is especially scenic between Waukegan and Evanston as it twists its way through some of the most expensive real estate in the Midwest.

[2]   In 1838, a group of Alsatian farmers from the Saar Valley settled in Lake County, about thirty miles northwest of the lakeside town of Chicago. The economic life of Long Grove centered around a crossroads, and when the village went into decline in the years after World War I, the crossroads settlement remained untouched. Antique-hunters discovered the place in the 1940s; now its nineteenth-century structures have become a charming commercial center for nostalgia-seekers. Zoning laws require that any new construction conform to the century-old style of the restoration.

[3]   The Baha'i Faith was founded in Iran in the mid-nineteenth century by the prophet Baha'u'llah, a young nobleman who left a life of ease to preach a doctrine of religious concord and unity. By 1894 Chicago had become the largest North American center of the faith, and plans were begun for construction of a House of Worship. The result is a fantasy in concrete tracery that rises off Sheridan Road in Wilmette. The nine-sided structure was designed by Louis Bourgeois and completed in 1929. The airy quality of the dome was achieved by mixing quartz and Portland cement within plaster molds and hanging them on a steel superstructure. The House of Worship and its surrounding gardens are open daily, 10:00 to 5:00, mid-October to mid-May; rest of the year, from 10:00 to 10:00. Services are held at 3:00 P.M. Sunday. There is no admission charge.

[4]   Northwestern University, one of the most prestigious institutions in the Midwest, has its main campus in Evanston, abutting Chicago's northern border. Part of its campus lies along the lakeshore, although its historic center, dating to 1855, is west of Sheridan Road. During the academic year, free walking tours are given at 2:00 P.M., Monday through Friday, and at noon on

Saturday. They leave from the Rebecca Crown Memorial Center at 633 Clark Street, three blocks west of Sheridan. Reservations should be made in advance by calling 492-7271.

[5]   For many years, Evanston was a center of the temperance movement and remained a dry town in deference to one of its leading residents, Frances Willard, founder of the National Women's Christian Temperance Union. Mrs. Willard's home at 1730 Chicago Avenue is now a WCTU museum exhibiting mementoes of her career and family. It is open Monday through Friday, 9:00 to 4:30 and by appointment on Saturday (call 864-1397). There is no admission charge.

[6]   Another notable Evanston resident was Charles G. Dawes, vice-president in the Calvin Coolidge administration. His twenty-eight-room house at 225 Greenwood Avenue is now the Evanston Historical Society. It is open from 1:00 to 5:00, except on Wednesday and Sunday. There is an admission charge.

[7]   Frank Lloyd Wright moved to Oak Park in 1889 as a twenty-two-year-old newlywed. For the next twenty years the town became a laboratory for his ideas on residential architecture as he worked toward development of the Prairie House. He redesigned his own home on the average of every eighteen months. Meanwhile, he began receiving commissions for new homes on the surrounding streets of the prosperous residential suburb. As a result, Oak Park and neighboring River Forest have the largest collection of Wright buildings in the world, a total of thirty-one structures. Among them is the Unity Temple, at 875 Lake Street, regarded as his first important public building and a pioneering effort in the use of poured concrete. The Wright home and studio, at Chicago and Forest avenues, are open for guided tours from 1:00 to 2:30 on Tuesday and Thursday, and 1:00 to 4:30 on Saturday and Sunday. There is an admission charge. The Unity Temple is open Tuesday, Thursday, and Friday, 1:00 to 5:00; Saturday and Sunday 2:00 to 3:00. In summer, the temple is open only Tuesday and weekends. There is an admission charge. The temple is also the starting point for walking tours of the Wright buildings on weekends at 2:00 P.M. There is a fee. For reservations, call 848-1978. Self-guided walking tours are easily arranged with the assistance of a pamphlet published by the Oak

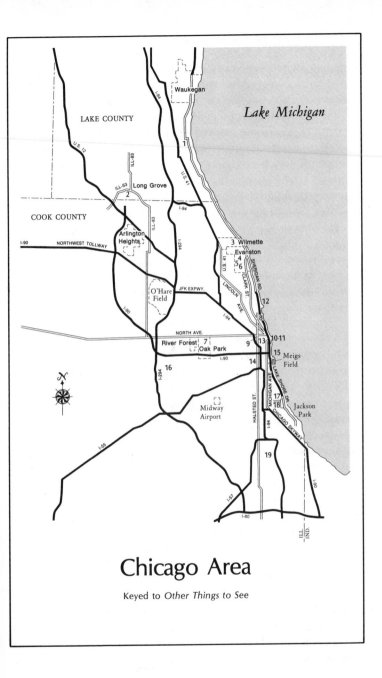

Chicago Area

Keyed to *Other Things to See*

Park Public Library, at 834 Lake Avenue. There is a charge for the pamphlet.

[8]   New Town is a shopping and entertainment district along Clark Street on Chicago's North Side. It was formed in the early 1970s. There are galleries, ethnic restaurants, offbeat taverns, and boutiques clustered in this strip running from about the 2400 to the 3400 block on Clark.

[9]   To the south of New Town is Old Town, a similar area that was developed a decade earlier along Wells Street. Old Town was one of the first nineteenth-century urban districts in the country to become a reborn entertainment area by taking advantage of its unique architecture and convenient location to the central city. Be sure to stroll along North Park and Lincoln Park West (the blocks to the west of Wells) to see the restored homes and townhouses, projects stimulated by the success of Old Town.

[10]   Navy Pier lies at the end of Grand Street, three blocks north of the Chicago River. The city-owned facility extends 3,000 feet into the lake and is the perfect spot for observing ships unloading their international cargoes at the Port of Chicago. It is open daily, 10:00 to 10:00. There is no admission charge.

[11]   To get even closer to the water, the Clipper Line runs steamboat excursions on the lake from Navy Pier daily, from Memorial Day weekend to mid-September. The cruises are of varying lengths and run from 10:00 A.M. to 11:30 P.M. On Friday and Saturday, a late cruise runs until 3:00 A.M. Call 329-1800 for current schedules. Cruises that concentrate on the Chicago River's course through the business district, as well as the lake, begin near the stairs descending to the water from the Wrigley Building at the Michigan Avenue Bridge. The Wendella cruises leave for varying lengths of time daily at 10:00, 1:15, 3:15, and 7:30, from mid-April to mid-September. Schedules are subject to change. Call 337-1446 for current information.

[12]   Lincoln Park is the glory of the North Side lakefront. It is a 1,000-acre facility that parallels the water from North Avenue all the way up to Hollywood Avenue, a stretch of about four miles. In its confines there are two museums, a zoo, a conservatory, a nine-hole golf course, several beaches, and recreational

facilities of all kinds. It is Chicago's weekend getaway with thousands of residents from the adjacent neighborhoods and beyond crowding in to play. The Chicago Historical Society Museum is described in the Gold Coast section of this chapter. The Chicago Academy of Sciences, at 2001 North Clark Street, concentrates on ecology and the environment of Chicago and the Great Lakes. It is open daily from 10:00 to 5:00. There is no admission charge. The zoo may be entered from either Webster Avenue or Fullerton Avenue, west of Lake Shore Drive. The thirty-five-acre facility includes a children's zoo and operating farm, but is best known for its Ape House with the largest zoo collection of great apes. They are placed in a tropical setting, with twice-daily simulated storms to heighten the effect. The zoo is open daily from 10:00 to 5:00. There is no admission charge. The Conservatory consists of four glassed buildings—the Palm House, Fernery, Tropical House, and Show House—as well as three outdoor gardens. Major shows are held in November, Christmas, late February, and Easter. The conservatory is open daily from 9:00 to 5:00, and until 9:00 P.M. during shows. There is no admission charge.

[13]   At its opening in 1930, the Merchandise Mart was the largest commercial structure in the world. It has lost that title, but still is an imposing piece of work and the largest wholesale center in the country. It hosts major trade shows throughout the year. Located at Wells Street on the north bank of the Chicago River, the Mart offers ninety-minute tours that start in its lobby every half hour from 9:30 to 3:30 on weekdays. There is a small charge. Another way of visiting the Mart is to tour the Quaker Oats test kitchens, a collection of modern kitchens with home economists demonstrating recipes and appliances. The free tours are held on week days from 9:30 to noon and from 1:30 to 3:30. Reservations should be made at 222-6809.

[14]   Hull House is a monument in the field of social work, the site of the landmark work done by Jane Addams at the turn of the century among Chicago's poor, immigrant population. Now a part of the University of Illinois–Chicago Circle campus at 800 South Halsted, Hull House has been restored and turned into a museum of the period and the person. It is open Monday through

Friday, 10:00 to 4:00 and on Sunday, 1:00 to 5:00. There is no admission charge.

[15]   The 1800 block of Prairie Avenue was Chicago's most elegant address in the last two decades of the nineteenth century. Now it is being restored to its former sheen. The Glessner House, at 1800 South Prairie, built in 1886 by Henry Hobson Richardson, is headquarters for both the project and the Chicago School of Architecture Foundation. The thirty-five-room home was built for a founder of the International Harvester Company and is noted for its use of windows opening onto a sheltered courtyard rather than the street. Tours of the house are given on Tuesday, Thursday, and Saturday, 10:00 to 4:00 and Sunday, 1:00 to 5:00. There is an admission charge. Other houses on the block are also being restored, including the Widow Clarke House, moved to the area from another location and believed to be the oldest residence in the city. It dates from 1837. The Chicago School Foundation offers a series of twenty-one walking tours of architecture throughout the city held at various times. For current schedule information call 326-1393 or inquire at the Glessner House.

[16]   The Chicago Zoological Park in suburban Brookfield is the largest such facility in the area, at 200 acres almost six times the size of the Lincoln Park Zoo. The big attraction here is the porpoise show in the Seven Seas Panorama. A miniature railroad makes a circuit of the grounds. It is open daily, 10:00 to 6:00, May to September; rest of the year until 5:00. There is an admission charge. It is located at Thirty-first Street and First Avenue in Brookfield, about eleven miles west of the Loop.

[17]   The University of Chicago has been one of the most influential and respected institutions in the country since its founding in 1891. It occupies a huge tract of land in the city's Hyde Park area on the South Side, west of Jackson Park between Fifty-sixth and Sixty-first streets. The Midway Plaisance, the original midway of the 1893 Columbian Exposition, is its main artery. Tours of the campus are given each Saturday at 10:00 A.M. from 1212 East Fifty-ninth Street. For a quick tour on your own, though, start at Woodlawn Avenue and Fifty-ninth Street at the Rockefeller Memorial Chapel. The university was founded by

John D. Rockefeller, and this chapel, a memorial to his mother, was completed in 1928 in full Gothic-revival regalia. The vaulted ceiling and the banners in the interior which were used in the Vatican Pavilion at the 1964 New York World's Fair are worth noting. Head north one block to Fifty-eighth; on the northeast corner is the Robie House, built by Frank Lloyd Wright in 1909 and regarded as the best example of his Prairie House architecture. The house was restored in 1967. The low roof line, wide eaves, and "bold interplay of horizontal mass" (in the words of the Chicago Landmarks Commission) typify this revolutionary form of domestic architecture. The house may be toured by appointment. Call 753-4429 for information. Walk west on Fifty-eighth for a block and you'll enter the Quadrangle, a three-block-square open area surrounded by many of the university's most impressive buildings. Leave by the western or Ellis Street side and head north across Fifty-seventh Street. In this area once stood the university football field; it was here that a team of scientists, led by Enrico Fermi, conducted the work that led to the atomic bomb. A bronze sculpture by Henry Moore, *Nuclear Energy,* now marks the site.

[18] Also on the university grounds is another of Chicago's excellent museums. The Oriental Institute, at Fifty-eighth and University streets, is a treasure house for those interested in the cultures of ancient Egypt and Mesopotamia. The University of Chicago has conducted extensive archaeological work in the Middle East since the 1920s, and this museum displays the fruits of it: winged bulls, mummies, Babylonian walls, and much more. The institute is open daily except Monday. Hours are 10:00 to 4:00; Sunday, noon to 4:00. There is no admission charge.

[19] A social experiment that ended in a disastrous strike has become one of Chicago's most interesting neighborhoods. Pullman was begun as a company town by the sleeping car firm in 1880. Its founder, George Pullman, believed that allowing workers to live in an ideal setting would increase productivity and loyalty. It was a prosperous, seemingly contented place with a population of 11,800. But when the depression of 1893 hit, Pullman refused to lower his rents and store prices, a grievance

committee was dismissed, and a company-wide strike involving violence and federal troops resulted. The courts ordered Pullman's company to divest itself of town properties, and the town became totally absorbed by the surrounding city in 1889. Today it is a fascinating area, a National Historic Landmark in utopian planning. The area is located east of Cottage Grove Avenue between 111th and 115th streets. Tours are given Monday through Friday at 1:30 P.M. from the Hotel Florence at 11111 South Forrestville Avenue, and the first Sunday of every month, May through October, at 1:30 from the Historic Pullman Center, 614 East 113th Street. The center has further information about other tour times.

Side Trips

Elgin, thirty-six miles northwest of Chicago on the Northwest Tollway, is an industrial town on the scenic Fox River. A ride along the Fox in old trolleys and interurban rail cars may be taken on the Fox River Line Railroad, in South Elgin, on Illinois 31. The twenty-minute rides operate on Saturday, from 1:00 to 5:00, and Sunday, from 11:00 to 6:00, August to October. In June and July they run on Sunday only, 11:00 to 6:00. There is an admission charge.

Batavia, thirty-seven miles west of Chicago on the East-West Tollway and Illinois 31, is the site of the Enrico Fermi National Accelerator Laboratory. A viewing area overlooking the world's largest proton accelerator may be visited during daylight hours, Monday through Friday. There is no admission charge.

Elmhurst, sixteen miles west of Chicago on Interstate 90, is the site of the Lizzadro Museum of Lapidary Art, the largest display of gems and jewelry in the country, in Wilder Park. There are closed-circuit televised demonstrations of gem-cutting. The museum is open Tuesday through Friday and on Sunday, 11:00 to 5:00; Saturday, 10:00 to 5:00. There is an admission charge.

Lisle, twenty-seven miles west of Chicago on the East-West Tollway, has the Morton Arboretum, at the Illinois 53 exit. This 1,500-acre park specializes in woody plants and also has a section of restored prairie. Grounds are open 9:00 to 5:00 during standard time, 9:00 to 7:00 during daylight saving time. There is a charge per car.

Lockport, thirty-five miles southwest of Chicago, on Interstate 55 and Illinois Highways 53 and 7, was headquarters for the canal that linked Chicago and the Mississippi River. Four canal locks remain in town, and the Old Canal Town National Historic District preserves many pre–Civil War buildings. A museum at 803 South State Street is open daily 1:00 to 4:30. There is no admission charge. Lockport holds an Old Canal Days celebration annually in the third week of June.

State Parks on the Lake

Illinois Beach State Park, 3 miles north of Waukegan, has a 3-mile-long sand beach, a lodge, and picnic areas. The 2,746-acre park has 440 campsites.

The city of Chicago has lined its lakefront with public beaches through its excellent system of parks. Major North Side beaches are Rogers Park and Loyola Park, just south of the Evanston boundary; Foster Avenue, Montrose-Wilson, and North Avenue in Lincoln Park; and Oak Street, just across Lake Shore Drive from the end of North Michigan Avenue. On the South Side, major beaches are located at Twelfth Street, Thirty-first Street, Forty-ninth Street, Fifty-seventh Street and Sixty-seventh Street; Rainbow Park in the Seventy-ninth Street area; and Calumet Park, just west of the Indiana state line. No camping is permitted in any of these city facilities.

Bibliography

Bach, Ira J. *Chicago on Foot*. Chicago: Rand McNally, 1977.

Bald, F. Clever. *Michigan in Four Centuries*. New York: Harper and Row, 1954.

————. *The Sault Canal Through 100 years*. Ann Arbor: University of Michigan Press, 1954.

Bayliss, Joseph E. and Estelle L. *River of Destiny: The St. Marys*. Detroit: Wayne State University Press, 1955.

Benedict, Harry C. *Red Metal*. Ann Arbor: University of Michigan Press, 1952.

Blegen, Theodore C. *Minnesota: A History of the State*. Minneapolis: University of Minnesota Press, 1975.

Brebner, J. Bartlet. *Canada: A Modern History*. Ann Arbor: University of Michigan Press, 1970.

Buley, Roscoe C. *The Old Northwest*. Indianapolis: Indiana Historical Society, 1950.

Channing, Edward. *The Story of the Great Lakes*. New York: Macmillan, 1912.

Colbert, Elias and Chamberlain, Everett. *Chicago and the Great Conflagration*. New York: Viking, 1971.

Cromie, Robert. *The Great Chicago Fire*. New York: McGraw-Hill, 1958.

Current, Richard N. *Wisconsin: A History*. New York: Norton, 1977.

Curwood, James O. *The Great Lakes*. New York: G. P. Putman's Sons, 1909.

Dedmon, Emmett. *Fabulous Chicago*. New York: Random House, 1953.

Dodge, Roy L. *Michigan Ghost Towns—Upper Peninsula*. Troy, Mich.: Glendon Publishers, 1973.

Fowle, Otto. *Sault Ste. Marie and Its Great Waterway*. New York: G. P. Putnam's Sons, 1925.

Gates, William B. *Michigan Copper and Boston Dollars*. Cambridge: Harvard University Press, 1951.

Gibbon, J. M. *Steel of Empire: The Canadian Pacific Railroad*. New York: Bobbs-Merrill, 1936.

Hatcher, Harlan H. *The Great Lakes*. New York: Oxford University Press, 1944.

Havighurst, Walter. *The Long Ships Passing*. New York: Macmillan, 1953.

Holbrook, Stewart H. *Iron Brew*. New York: Macmillan, 1939.

Holmquist, June D. *Minnesota's Major Historic Sites*. St. Paul: Minnesota Historical Society, 1963.

Hough, Jack L. *Geology of the Great Lakes*. Champaign: University of Illinois Press, 1958.

Inland Seas, Quarterly Journal of the Great Lakes Historical Society, Cleveland.

Jamison, James K. *This Ontonagon Country*. Ontonagon, Mich.: Ontonagon Herald Company, 1948.

Lass, William E. *Minnesota: A History*. New York: Norton, 1977.

McKee, Russell. *Great Lakes Country*. New York: Crowell, 1966.

Michigan: A Guide to the Wolverine State. New York: Oxford University Press, 1956.

Michigan History. Magazine of the Michigan Historical Commission, Lansing.

Murdoch, Angus. *Boom Copper*. New York: Macmillan, 1943.

Nesbit, Robert C. *A History of Wisconsin*. Madison: University of Wisconsin Press, 1973.

Nute, Grace Lee. *Lake Superior*. Indianapolis: Bobbs-Merrill, 1944.

———. *The Voyageurs' Highway*. St. Paul: Minnesota Historical Society, 1941.

Putnam, Donald F. *A Regional Geography of Canada*. Toronto: M. Dent and Sons, 1956.

Quaife, Milo M. *Chicago and the Old Northwest*. Chicago: University of Chicago Press, 1913.

———. *Lake Michigan*. Indianapolis: Bobbs-Merrill, 1944.

Rintala, Edsel K. *Douglass Houghton, Michigan's Pioneer Geologist*. Detroit: Wayne State University Press, 1954.

Shelton, Napier. *The Life of Isle Royale*. Washington: National Park Service, U.S. Department of the Interior, 1975.

Still, Bayrd. *Milwaukee, the History of a City*. Madison: State Historical Society of Wisconsin, 1948.

Wells, Robert W. *This Is Milwaukee*. Garden City, N.Y.: Doubleday, 1970.

Index

Conversion Chart

Because the metric system is presently in use in Canada and because the United States is in the process of converting to the metric system, the following chart is provided for your convenience.

> 1 inch = 2.54 centimeters
> 1 foot = 0.304 meters
> 1 mile = 1.6 kilometers
> 1 square mile = 2.59 square kilometers
> 1 acre = 0.405 hectares
> 1 gallon = 3.75 liters